JP Coelho

CW00687501

37

HACKS FOR PERSONAL GROWTH

37 HACKS FOR PERSONAL GROWTH

Life-Changing Ideas
in An Exhilarating Sketch
inspired by the **World's Highest Achievers in Fun, Graphic & Readable Format**

"Finally you'll finish a Non-Fiction Book!! if you don't finish the Book (in 20 years) Money Back Guaranteed

JP Coelho

#004

INDEX

#005

There are many famous quotes in this book, read them slowly (they were carefully handpicked) and PLEASE take your time to **contemplate the sketches and illustrations** by **Cat Rao**, an incredible artist!
Thank you for your work in this Book!

Cat Rao: Visual Development Artist, Colour Key artist and Character Designer follow
www.instagram.com/cat.rao
https://catraopajamas.com

00. INTRODUCTION

Oh no, not another motivational book!!
Yes, indeed, we have to do this.

This book was conceived from of a
simple question.
WHY are motivational books so Boring?

For years I would handout books to many friends – books that had an amazing effect on me personally. I gave many of these books away only to discover later that 90% of them were NEVER ever read!
Books that had the potential to change one's life but never made it beyond page 10!
That's when I decided to take matters into my own hands.
Would a compilation of all that these top achievers and gurus had written, presented in an easier way, make a book so easy and pleasant to read that, who knows, you might even read it until the very last page ?
Most of the content includes topics in areas where I would love to improve myself on a daily basis.
I consider the points below, mostly, as

NOTES TO SELF

because I want, and need, to improve in all the areas I have covered.

All the chapters could have included much more content, but I chose not to go that way and just throw in the "seeds". Chapters are short with lots of pictures, quotes, photos and some jokes (fingers crossed!).

It's kind of curious that a motivational book could be so "demotivating". When facing one of those boring 500-page motivational books, you need some tough resilience to finish it. Ironic, since that kind of person is exactly the sort who probably wouldn't need a motivational book!

Some chapters you might enjoy , others not so much, but the goal here is not that you love everything, or even try all the ideas. If you buy into some of the concepts, I will have the feeling of "mission accomplished" and my job is complete.
Feel free to e-mail me (joaopc@ onyriaresorts.com) with the quote that had most effect on you.
Intentionally, you will find repetitions and comments with slightly different angles. There are things that we only internalise having read them several times.
(there are lectures and podcasts that I have heard more than 20 times!)

"**Everything that needs to be said has already been said. But since no one was listening, must be said again**"

Andre Eide

#009

All the exceptional people mentioned in this book, I strongly advise you to read their books or listen to their podcasts because, by my calculation, they are approximately 70 times better than me!

Right, there are 2 things that I am sure of:
1- You will not live forever (and the world deserves to see your true potential ASAP)
2- You will finish this book (and really try some of these things)
You might ask, How can you be so sure of yourself?
You Won't Quit, BECAUSE YOU ARE NOT A LOSER!!
A Winner NEVER Quits & a Quitter NEVER Wins!

OK, if there is one thing I already know about you is that, you are NOT a loser ☺ at least not as much as this:
-You are such a loser! If there was contest for losers you would be 2nd!!
-Why not first?
-Because you are a LOSER!

About me

I am João, one of 6 brothers. I have a twin brother, born on August 7, 1979 in Lisbon and grew up and live in a lovely town called Cascais (30 minutes from Lisbon; more about Cascais in my blog: www.LocalCascais.com).
Proudly being Portuguese, people who from the 15th century with around 1 million inhabitants discovered the 4 corners of the world in small boats. Our people stayed in China, in Macau until 1999, introduced tempura to Japan, chili to India, and we even played a part in "afternoon tea" in England!
I would love to follow that Portuguese legacy, but sadly, I have a really hard time holding sushi chopsticks, can't handle spicy food and prefer beer to tea!
Not everything is lost. I do maintain the old Portuguese passion for travel, and love to make new friends everywhere.

António (twin brother)

My cousin, Bernardo

João (me)

#011

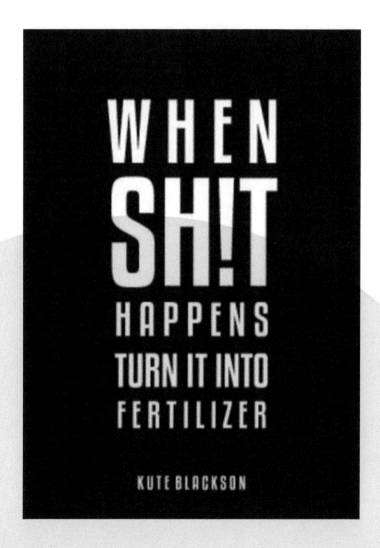

WHEN SH!T HAPPENS
TURN IT INTO FERTILIZER

KUTE BLACKSON

"You don't have to be great to start, but you have to start to be great"

Zig Ziglar

Let's go!

Growing up, my brothers and I were extremely lucky to have a father who provided us with everything - much more than we ever deserved. When we got to our teenage years my father decided never to contribute €1 for all the fun things in life, including parties!. So we worked every summer to finance these important activities. We worked on the front-desk, did a bit of cleaning and even golf course irrigation! With the salary (which was dreadful!) we had great time during those summers with friends.

At one of those traditional festivals, I saw a fisherman walking towards me with an aggressive look on his face. Without hesitation, he punched me hard, enough to leave me knocked out lying on the floor. I got up and ran to tell my brother thinking that maybe we could get our own back. António laughed and replied: "Don't worry. Everything is sorted between the fisherman and I!"

The fundamental purpose of writing this book is to contribute some ideas on how to become the best version of yourself.
(Of course, I also have an ambition to look good on social media too - at least for a day!)

For me, the joy of everyday life is a natural consequence of making the best of ALL situations and not taking ourselves too seriously.

But
WHY 37 HACKS
and not 38 or 39??

First, because that's where I decided to stop, and this is MY book, so I make the rules around here!

Also, when I was almost done, I looked to see if there was some kind of meaning behind number 37, and look what I found:

"The number 37 symbolizes things like exploration, introspection, creativity, independence, self-determination and self-expression.

It relates to people who enjoy exploring new locations, new ideas, things, methods."

Coincidence ? I don't think so ☺

Seven years ago my TV at home stopped working, because I can be sometimes a bit lazy, I did nothing about it. Soon, I realised that I didn't need a TV. It was a waste of time.

Three things I realized after **seven** years without TV:

1 - The number of "self-improvement" books increased massively
2 - I improved, personally, in many areas of my life (and realized I can improve much more!)
3 - Reading those books was difficult.

Reading this book will be EASY - a walk in the park - as you already know everything about these 37 Hacks. The objective here was to write this in such a way that would make you smile, laugh or even feel guilty and bad about yourself. Whenever there is some degree of emotion involved, you WILL remember it. This approach was intentional to make sure you remember and increase the odds of really trying this stuff to make your life better (and more fun!).

A helpful piece of advice - **read this book slowly and repeat it whenever you feel uninspired!**

PEOPLE OFTEN SAY THAT
MOTIVATION DOESN'T LAST.
WELL, NEITHER DOES BATHING.
THAT'S WHY WE RECOMMEND
IT DAILY.
ZIG ZIGLAR

#015

01. NO COMPLAINING

"DO THE BEST, WITH WHAT YOU HAVE, NOW!!"

- In your JOB!

Unless you are working for Google or Apple, it is unlikely that you will love everything about your job!

You either want more money, less hours, more exciting work, a nicer boss, or younger colleagues!

  (if you want more of all, please quit or seek assistance)

Life isn't perfect. That is why we call it "work" instead of "play".

Whatever job you have, focus on it and identify the parts you like.

There is always something nice to discover, even if it's just the canteen food or the dishy colleague in HR department!

Maybe you want more money, but you are learning a lot and networking with people who can lead you to exciting opportunities for the future.

Stay positive and search for alternatives while maintaining a good professional image!

Don't complain. Many people would like your job. Do your best while you have it.

- At RESTAURANTS

Don't allow a bad experience in a restaurant ruin your mood

 (and the mood of the people who are with you!)

During a summer holiday, if my friends and I found ourselves stuck in a really bad restaurant, we tended to go back there for a couple of times.

We were laughing and enjoying the fiasco!!

THERE ARE PEOPLE WHO WOULD LOVE TO HAVE YOUR BAD DAYS.

>>

Don't complain, you are lucky somebody is cooking for you (or trying to cook)!

- In SPORTS
In sports, historically, I always had a bad temper.
One day, on the golf course, something happened that changed my perspective forever. Playing golf in the Algarve, against my twin brother, and with my cousin Bernardo who joined us in a buggy to watch us play.
(these days, my cousin can't play anymore because he has ALS sclerosis , but he used to be a brilliant golfer with single figure handicap) .
Towards the end I hit a bad shot way too far left; I got angry and frustrated threw the club whilst screaming some very bad language (not for my mum's ears!)
My cousin was staring at me and said: "Calm down Joao - I only wish I was able to hit a golf ball again."
(Amazing how far I could throw golf clubs when I was angry; big improvement, Thanks also to Zen Golf Book – Joseph Parent ☺)

"When You Complain, Nobody Wants To Help You

Stephen Hawking

'Don't find fault, find a remedy; anybody can complain' Henry Ford

Don't complain about things you aren't willing to change Don't complain, just work harder

Jackie Robinson, had it in his contract, not to complain if people spit on him

02. NO EXCUSES

"THE FIRST SIGN OF A LOSER, IS AN EXCUSE!!"

Les Brown

It is always so easy to find excuses. If you get used to it, you might even become a specialist.

HE IS 104 YEARS OLD.
WHAT'S YOUR EXCUSE?

"He had more time to train"

When I started training for the very challenging IronMan triathlon, I got myself a coach. He was an excellent tutor who believed in hard work and no excuses. in short, he was the right man to help me because I was terrified!

I started to follow a strict training routine, always trying to look like a tough guy, but also to not let my coach down. One day, while cycling with a friend through the rain, I fell to the floor and suffered two ugly wounds to my leg and arm.

#022

I was in a bad way and I sent a text message to the coach: "I fell off the bike"
Coach answered: "Is the bike okay?"
I laughed, and I thought to myself: "hey, coach, don't worry about me!!"
That message couldn't be clearer:
NO EXCUSES!!!

It was the beginning of an enriching course of discipline. No excuses, and that is very important to me.

RULE #76:
NO EXCUSES,
PLAY LIKE A
CHAMPION

(Vince Vaughn & Owen Wilson @ Wedding Crashers Movie)

s it raining? You step outside and make that run!!

ead Tony Robbins book: A father, criminal, ug addict and alcoholic, he spent many ears in jail. He had two children, 11 months art. One of them was a success and had a eautiful family. The other followed the same iminal path as his father.
'hen they were asked, separately, why they ade those choices, the answer was the same om both of them.

With a father like that, had no choice!"

Michael Jackson: Lived with 11 people in a house with 2 bedrooms and 1 WC

Lionel Messi: Childhood diagnosed with autism and suffered dwarfism

#023

#024

What happens to us, in the past, can either be an excuse to remain the same, or a motivation to change.

From the Book "David & Goliath" by Malcom Gladwell: Underdogs, Misfits, and the Art of Battling Giants. In this great book Gladwell gives so many real examples of how several people have made an apparent disadvantage or handicap into a source of success.

Cristiano Ronaldo: father with drinking problem

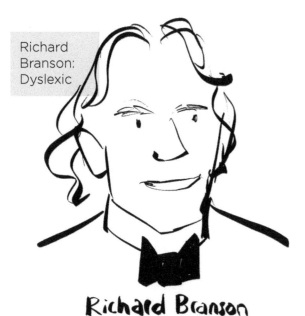

Richard Branson: Dyslexic

Richard Branson

Ed Sheeran: Bulling target (ugly + lazy eye & severe speech problems)

"Losers Make Excuses, Champions Make Adjustments"

Les Brown

NAME:	This was NOT an Excuse:	Celebrated Worldwide as:
Nick Vujicic	Born without Arms and legs	motivational speaker
Ludwig van Beethoven	Deaf , alcoholic father	pianist and composer
Marla Runyan	Blind	Olympic marathon runner
Stephen Hawking	Amyotrophic Lateral Sclerosis (ALS)	physicist, cosmologist
Bethany Hamilton	Lost her arm in a shark attack in Hawaii, aged 13.	surfer

It all comes down to how we interpret what happens to us. We can choose a negative interpretation and use that as an excuse - our reason for not being able to achieve our goals.
Or we can use remarkable events as a wakeup call, as an opportunity to show that we are strong, have an opportunity to grow, to make our mark and inspire others (like us) not to be sissies.

"It's all about the Story you tell Yourself"

It's no coincidence that most successful people had, at some point in their lives, great challenges. As Tony Robbins says, the story we tell ourselves dictates our destiny.

The names above could also tell themselves a story:

"My father was nothing but a drunk, so I never managed to be anyone"
"I am deaf, so it's impossible to compose music"
"I am dyslexic, so I will never triumph as a businessman"

It would be the easiest way to go on repeating this story throughout life, and to become increasingly unhappy, poor and isolated.

The only thing standing between you and your goal is the bullshit story you keep telling yourself as to why you can't achieve it.
-The Wolf of Wall Street

Motivational Speaker, Eric Thomas, repeats often:
"My Greatest Asset is that I was Homeless, So I don't feel any pain"

I guess we are back to the same thing:
"you Either have Excuses or Results"
➞ your decision now!

Losers are the "champions"... of excuses (been there 😊). Winners triumph despite difficult circumstances and disadvantageous backgrounds (which, by the way, helped them to become stronger). True champions know that they will very rarely have a battle in the perfect circumstances!

"Adversity introduces a Man to Himself"

Albert Einstein

It's cold and raining? go practice outside anyway!
Your colleague is the boss's best friend? → just do the extra mile every day and surprise everybody!
Do you live far from your work? → start listening to podcasts and learning something new daily!

Problems are your greatest opportunity to show that you are different and that you are not someone who is always waiting to get help from others.
Speaking of whining, it makes sense to recall a phrase that my father used to say when i whinged about struggling to close sales back in 2008:

In times of crisis some people cry and others sell handkerchiefs

For those who like music it is also worth remembering:
The legendary guitarist from **Black Sabbath,** Tony Iommi, lost the tips of two fingers of his right hand in a factory accident. This severely affected his playing style! Nevertheless, Tony was ranked nº25 by Rolling Stone Magazine in the list of the **"100 Greatest Guitarists of All Time"**
Another guitarist from **Grateful Dead**, Jerry Garcia, lost two thirds of his middle finger on his right hand in an accident when he was just 4 years old. That may have prevented Jerry from making obscene gestures during road rage incidents, but it didn't stop him from becoming a great guitarist and taking his band to the **Rock and Roll Hall of Fame** - selling over **35 million albums worldwide!**

Tony Iommi -
Black Sabbath

#027

There are no excuses!!
...but don't do something stupid to your hand)

03. DON'T TAKE YOURSELF SERIOUSLY

The only way to evolve is by stepping out of your comfort zone (no apology for the cliché!). When we are out of our comfort zone, we probably won't exude great style. We might even look ridiculous.
But if we take ourselves too seriously, we won't evolve because we will never try new things. (and remember, people who take themselves too seriously are usually quite dull!!)

Entrepreneur Sam Walton, who started with just a small Wal-Mart store and then developed a $44 billion empire, once said:

"Celebrate your successes: find some humour in your failures"

Only with this spirit can one grow, try new things, and maintain some sanity.

Tennis player Vitas Gerulaitis lost 16 times in a row against Jimmy Connors.
The 17th time they played, Vitas finally won, and said:

"NOBODY BEATS VITAS GERULAITIS 17 TIMES IN A ROW"

When it comes to tennis I can tell you about someone who takes himself quite seriously - my brother!
He regularly plays tennis with his father-in-law and always beats him by 6-0 6-0!

From the movie "Dumb & Dumber":
Mary says: **"your chances are more like 1 in a million!"**
Lloyd answers **"So you are telling me there IS a chance!!"**

"Sansego" is a great community for triathletes to help them reach the next level! (with the help of great professionals and champions like Craig Alexander, 5 times triathlon World Champion)
"Sansego" is their lifestyle mantra - it means To live Sans (without) Ego!
It's a wonderful mantra, When we forget about our ego we are open to try out new things, and are not scared of what others will think, or looking ridiculous, and have more freedom!
When your ego gets in the way we become blind and small.
While we're on the subject of "not being scared of looking ridiculous", here is my singing "performance" at a friend's wedding.

#029

"**"EVERY DAY YOU EITHER IMPROVE OR GET WORSE, BUT YOU NEVER STAY THE SAME!"**

Bo Schembechler, legendary coach, NFL

04. CONSTANT & NEVER-ENDING IMPROVEMENT

All the big winners in sport, music, science, and business are addicted to self-improvement and never waste a minute.

Cristiano Ronaldo himself went to practice alone the day after winning the Ballon d'Or! (Of all the players who attended that awards gala dinner, Cristiano was the only one who practiced. No wonder he continued to accumulate so many awards!). Their secret is that they fall in love with the process, and they love to practice.
The greatest motivating force that can exist is perceived progress. Seeing progress, however small, is highly motivating and keeps us going.

Tony Robbins goes further and says
"Progress equals Happiness"
It makes perfect sense. Whenever we are growing and progressing, we look forward to tomorrow!

DO SOMETHING EVERYDAY THAT BRINGS YOU CLOSER TO YOUR GOALS!

#031

05. MEDITATION

Meditation always sounded a bit ridiculous to me. I had images of a guy dressed like the Dalai Lama sat in top of a mountain in Tibet. Recently I discovered that even a company like Google had an department dedicated to this called: "Search Inside Yourself". It was time to investigate further. Trust me - usually these geeks know a lot more than we do!
I discovered that many successful people (including those I admire for different reasons) are very active in meditation. But most don't look like Buddhist Monks!

- Richard Gere - Jennifer Aniston,

- Angeline Jolie - Clint Eastwood,

- Sir Paul McCartney - Kobe Bryant,

- Jerry Seinfeld - Keanu Reeves,

- Madonna - Eva Mendes,

- Oprah Winfrey- Steve Jobs

- Kate Perry - Gisele Bundchen

- Cameron Diaz - Jennifer Lopez,

- Sting , etc etc

THE ART OF RESTING THE MIND AND THE POWER OF DISMISSING FROM IT ALL CARE AND WORRY IS PROBABLY ONE OF THE SECRETS OF OUR GREAT MEN.
CAPTAIN J. A. HATFIELD.

I guess Tim (Ferris) is right again. In his book "Tools of Titans, he finds that **80% of the high achievers** he interviewed **do some kind of daily mindfulness practice or meditation...**

Apps like **Calm** or **HeadSpace** will do everything for you if you decide to commit 5-10 minutes a day.

Is not an understatement either if we say that meditation can be the key to happiness.
Meditation helps you to be in the "present".
If you don't find some form of meditation (it could be gardening, walking your dog or even a sauna with controlled breathing) you will never be enjoying the "present" moment. You will be always thinking about the future, or dwelling on the past.
And when the next moment arrives, you will do it again and again! (not to mention - even worse - the times

when we stay stuck in the past, killing off all potential progress and suffering unnecessarily)

Meditation is a great way to discipline our emotions. When we are at the mercy of our emotions, we make a lot of mistakes (my list of mistakes is HUGE!).

> **"Learn to discipline your emotions because if you don't, your enemies will use them against you."**
>
> Bruce Lee

#033

Although I am already collecting some nice rewards from my meditation process, I still consider myself to be a beginner, so I will recommend two books that increased my interest in this life changing routine:
- **Zen Habits – Leo Babauta**
- **CALM: Calm the Mind. Change the World – Michael Acton Smith**

There are many forms of meditation. What is absolutely key is to make time for some ALONE TIME! Its crucial to have time to shut down. Learning to enjoy our own's company is the best way to recharge your batteries, clear your mind and let go of the stress of our daily lives.

Early mornings is a FANTASTIC time of the day for this Alone Time/Meditation. Many high achievers choose that time of the day because they know NOBODY can bother them. (even if you have five kids!)

My Brother Antonio has a well-established meditation routine, and has now reached more than 1,000 "meditation mornings". So he got to the point where felt entitled to brag about his "new me" - a much calmer person who would not get irritated easily.
His big glory moment was when he was in the car with his daughter in a lot of traffic and she asked why the car horn never works in daddy´s car!
One morning when he thought he was alone, he poured himself a glass of water. The glass slipped and smashed on the floor.
He started cursing BIG time "Fuc--- ; Fuc--- ; fuc---"!
That was the moment his daughter came in and said:
- Daddy, you forgot to do your meditation!!
(By the way, this girl´s school has meditation classes for kids from 6 years old #SomeHopeForTheFuture)

"**God grant me the Serenity to accept the things I cannot change, the Courage to change the things I can, and the Wisdom to know the difference.**"

Reinhold Niebuhr

06. TAKE YOUR HABITS SERIOUSLY

I have said before "don't take yourself too seriously" but when it comes to HABITS you need to take them very seriously. Here is why:

"HABITS WILL FORM WHETHER YOU WANT THEM OR NOT. WHATEVER YOU REPEAT, YOU REINFORCE"

James Clear

An excellent book about habits that I love is "Atomic Habits" by James Clear. I like it mainly because it has practical tips to stop some habits that I have and don't like (i.e addiction to social media) and also tips to start implementing some new habits.

> **"If you can replace a bad habit with a good one, you'll live with the benefits for decades. "**
>
> Seth Godin

Habits don't always have short-term results, but in the medium and long term the accumulation of those small decisions define the people we become. Author Simon Sinek uses a very visual analogy:

"What does brushing your teeth for 2 minutes achieve?
Absolutely nothing unless you do it twice a day, every day.

It´s the consistency. The accumulation of brushing your teeth day after day that protects them and prevents them from falling out.
If one day you go for a 5 hour run, and do nothing else, when summer arrives you will still be out of shape.
But if you run for 20 minutes every day, you'll be in great shape by the time summer comes.
The starting point is to look at our daily routines and think about our habits,

...host of which we do on "autopilot". Are these ...abits helping or harming us?

...re these habits bringing us closer ...o, or further away, from our goals?

...ur great victories and defeats, our amazing ...ob promotion or the day we got fired – all are a ...esult of many small and repeated actions. ...hese small daily routines (good or bad) and ...mall daily rituals (good or bad) are what bring ...s closer or push us further away from the ...eople we want to be tomorrow.

...If I keep eating those donuts **every morning**, ...will I be in great shape for the summer? ...If on the way to work, **every day**, I listen to ...15 minutes of a podcast about my area, do I ...become stupid? ...when I get home, **every day**, instead of those ...30-minutes scrolling social media I start taking ...a 30-minute run, do I get a bigger belly?

Sometimes the best way to end a bad habit is to replace it with another habit (a good one, please).
Many people after a moment of stress think that they really need to smoke a cigarette, when it could be replaced by a short walk taking some deep breaths. (Personally, when I wanted to do more sports and drink less beer, I noticed that the real addiction I had was actually having a glass in my hand.)

»

...ERIOUSLY

One of the tips I started using from the book "Atomic Habits" to stop some bad habits was:

"Cut out as many triggers as possible."

It is pretty simple, and it works!
If you continue to have a house full of cookies it will be difficult to stop eating them. It's far easier if you start buying fruit and keep that in the fridge instead!
When you go to bed leave your cell phone in the living room. It will be much easier to forget about it.
Other habits that we want to change may also be easier if we join forces with someone. If you agree to run at the end of the day with a friend, it becomes more difficult to cancel.
-During your lunch break, instead of always eating what you like, start going to the gym or taking a walk to relax? Convince your regular lunch partner to join you.
You don't need to waste your money on a clairvoyant to predict your future. If we know someone's routines, schedules and habits, we can very easily predict whether they will succeed or not.

We become what we repeatedly do
Sean Covey

(*) a Man went to a Witch to find out about his future.
When he arrived, he knocked on the door and the Witch asked:
Who is this?
The Man replied very angrily:
"This is NOT a good start!"

07. LISTEN MORE (& MORE)

Of all the things that are written in this book, here is one that I find VERY difficult...
To shut up and listen!
There are a thousand reasons why we should listen more than speak, starting with the obvious **"For some reason, we have two ears and only one mouth"**

Whenever we brag about an achievement, the probability of someone listening who is a higher achiever than us is quite large.
Many times I made a fool of myself by bragging about something and, then someone tells me that they have done even better. And still, I do the same thing again!

»

#039

#040

We always look better when we remember that:
"TO BE INTERESTING YOU HAVE TO BE INTERESTED!" = LISTEN, LISTEN, LISTEN!!!

The famous painter Pablo Picasso was known for sucking information and energy from the people he knew! No wonder he had plenty of material for creative inspiration.

Many years ago, at the hotel where I worked, a competitor of ours paid us a visit. He was "just" the owner of the largest hotel chain in the country. He asked me to show him the renovations we had just done at our hotel, and I was obviously happy to oblige. Throughout the visit he asked me a thousand questions about everything to do with our hotel - costs, performance, markets etc.
Only when he left did I realize that I had passed up an excellent opportunity to learn something myself from the country's leading hotelier. I had just rambled on giving him lots of information.
That same year I had the unique opportunity to play 18 holes with the charismatic rock legend **Alice Cooper.**
Having learned my lesson, I bombarded Alice Cooper with a thousand questions about music, his life, what he listened to in the car, other famous people he knew - everything!!
I think at the end, even after beating me on the golf course, Alice Cooper was a bit tired of me 😊
(By the way, he told me he listens to The Beatles in his car!)

November 2010, playing golf with Alice Cooper @ Quinta da Marinha – I was a bit heavier and hairier!

Note to self. SHUT up and listen!!

Simon Sinek, author of several best-selling books like **"Start with Why"** adds that besides the crucial part of **listening + listening + listening,** it is essential also to **speak LAST!**
(a trick Nelson Mandela learned from his father in the South African tribes)
If we listen well and wait to speak only at the very end, we will have a broader perspective and the other person will also truly digest what we say.

I JUST WANT
YOU TO LISTEN
TO ME BITCH
ABOUT IT...

How many times do we speak out of turn and it makes our our situation worse? One of Simon Sinek's excellent books is called **"Leaders Eat Last"** but I always think it would be also suit to have an alternative title: **"Leaders Speak Last"**!

More stuff on this topic, inspired by Austin Kleon: Pay attention 😊:

-- **Attention is the most precious thing we have - that's why everyone tries to steal it. (even your mother!!!)**
-- **Giving attention is the most basic proof of love.** 🖤
-- **If you want to change your life, start paying attention to other things (including people).**

By the way, it's OK to "Unfollow" people in real life!!

"Tell me what you pay attention to, I will tell you who you are"

Jose Ortega y Gasset

#041

08. INVEST IN YOURSELF

"EVERYONE IS A SELF-MADE MAN. ONLY THE SUCCESSFUL ADMIT IT"

Will Rogers

1

1 hour per day or even ½ hour
(can even be in the traffic jams; listening music, podcasts, etc)

(I am against Guns but if you have one at home, go get it and shoot your TV)

"FORMAL EDUCATION WILL MAKE YOU A LIVING, SELF-EDUCATION WILL MAKE YOU A FORTUNE"

Jim Rohn

IMAGINE 1 HOUR PER DAY DOING THIS (OR A MIX OF THEM):

- Learn anecdotes .Read consistently
- Write poems to your wife 😊
- Make-up tutorial
- Memorize cheesy & hilarious "pick-up" lines
- CrossFit or SpinBike
- Practice Reggaeton's steps
- Watch movies in Spanish. Listen to French music
- Practice golf (short-game)
- Sing (please be careful!)
- Swim

- Cook Italian food
- Podcasts on x or Audiobooks about y
- Learn to play guitar with your son or nephew
- Read one short story to your son per day
- Meditate / Flex
- Catch flies with chopsticks just like the Karate Kid and Sensei Mr Miyagi!
- Learn to down a beer fast 😊
- Join a painting class on YouTube
- Gardening

"Lack of time is lack of priorities"

"I don't have time" is a sentence that we hear so many times and, we all know, it's just a lame excuse!!
(the lock-down time during the Covid19 crisis showed that time is not the problem).
Please, never say you don't have 30 minutes per day to do something that effectively improves your life! Because later you will be spending 30-40 minutes per day on social media, just checking other peoples' lives, plus 45 minutes per day in front of your TV channel-hopping without watching anything interesting.

"Every day do something that will inch you closer to a better tomorrow"

Doug Firebaugh

Imagine the difference that 30 to 45 minutes per day x 300 days per year invested in your body or head or a specific skill!
(I'm already being generous.... giving you 65 days off!)

This 30 to 45 minute investment can make a HUGE difference in some area that is really important to you, and have a HUGE impact on improving your life!

- Want to be a better parent? (or do you prefer to pay fortunes to private tutors while crossing fingers it all turns out OK?)
- Want to be a better sportsman and beat that annoying guy?
- Want to learn a new hobby ?

30 minutes per day EXERCISE = less than 20 kilos / half-marathon / six pack

30 minutes per day MEDITATION = inner peace for situations that might have been exhausting

30 minutes per day READING = 20 books per year; specialising in any area you can dream of!

30 minutes per day in WRITING = publish a book/ become an opinion leader/ respected blogger

30 minutes per day in NEW HOBBY (*) = Music, painting, brewing your own beer at home!

OR, Continue with your 30 minutes per day on TV = become a specialist on reality TV shows...

(*) – if you want to learn any new hobby faster read **"the first 20 hours - Josh Kaufman"**

"AFRAID OF CHANGE?? NO!! AFRAID TO CONTINUE THE SAME!"

I really didn't want to show-off, but here lies a great opportunity 😊.
Using that daily time that normally used to be useless for me (TV, Social Media), I already accomplished some nice things:

- **I ran a marathon**
- **I read consistently more than 15 books per year**
- **I took music lessons (without good results but it was fun!)**
- **I meditated**
- **I did an IronMan Triathlon**
- **I am writing this** ☺

PLEASE set your priorities and go. Attack now!
(or continue on watching TV and scrolling Social media)

The Italian, **Gabriele D´Annunzio (1863-1938)**, was short, ugly, bald, unhealthy teeth and had lots of debts (he often went bankrupt) yet was considered one of the biggest seducers of all time.
"D´Annunzio was so widely desired that "the women who had not slept with him became laughing stock"*
(* New York Post)

Consistency is the name of the game!!

Returning to **Gabriele D´Annunzio**, he had horrible teeth, unlike ourselves who spend 5 minutes per day brushing our teeth over a period of many years.
Those ugly teeth were a big clue, the tip of the iceberg, of a life without any discipline.
Gabriele D´Annunzio had a big talent, no doubt. Enough to give him some fun but not enough to prevent him from going to jail or going bankrupt many times.
Quite sad because he could easily have become legendary in many parts of his life, instead of just one ...

09. EXERCISE

> "TAKE CARE OF YOUR BODY. IT'S THE ONLY PLACE YOU HAVE TO LIVE."
>
> Jim Rohn

Don't worry, I won't write about the benefits of exercise to your health or self-esteem! We all know the huge rewards from exercising on regular basis.

We all prefer to lie on the beach or have a beer, instead of going for a run or doing some press-ups.
We all prefer to stay in bed for an extra, 30 minutes rather than going outside for a run on a cold morning.

Even the great Mohammed Ali said:
"I hated every minute of training, but I said, 'Don't quit. Suffer now and live the rest of your life as a champion."

But it is common knowledge that nothing good in life can be achieved without some suffering. We have known this for over 2000 years. It has been written in the doctrines of all religions! Cross that desert to reach the promised land!

Inspired by the Book: **"Discipline Equals Freedom"** by Jocko Willink (follow Jocko´s Instagram, he wakes up EVERY day at 4:30 am).

These sacrifices open incredible doors. And whoever lacks discipline, sooner or later, will be trapped in a little world with no doors to open.
That's why it makes perfect sense when Jocko says:

"Discipline is your best friend!"

If you follow that path, discipline will give you the best life ever!

But how can we do it consistently?
You need some techniques and tricks to kick-start your exercise routine so that it becomes an automatic habit.

Willink

(more: https://www.spongecoach.com/best-jocko-willink-quotes/)

"THERE IS NO SUCH THING AS A WEEKEND. THIS IS AN EVERYDAY GIG. EVERY DAY IS A MONDAY"

Jocko Willink

#049

17 ideas that have worked incredibly well, for MANY people:

01 - Make it **FUN** (even if it is dancing classes of Kizomba)

02 - Create a **CHALLENGE** (sign up for 10km fun run)

03 - Find an **EXERCISE BUDDY** or even personal trainer you fancy ☺

04 - Give yourself a **REWARD** after exercising
(4 rewards that work for me: an extra-long shower, a sauna, diving in the sea, eating a lot of gelatin)

05 - Finish your exercising session when you are still feeling good (next time, before you start you training, you will have great memories from last session)

06 - Use your lunch break

07 - Use **MUSIC** (I didn't like to swim until I found the waterproof headphones ; Rocky's "Eye Of The Tiger" always does the trick)

08 - **Exercising Without Exercising** (Cycle to work / park your car far away and walk / leave one bus stop early/ use the stairs/ walk your dog/ walk during phone calls/ gardening/ clean the house, the dishes, your car)

09 - Find **SYNERGIES with other purposes** (running to spend time with the kids, run alongside your kids while they're cycling; running to meditate)

10 - **Start very slowly** and pretend you are only going to do a 10 minute session (95% of the time it will be + 30 minutes)

11 - **Preparing any equipment the night before** (helps a lot to visualise)

12 - Have a calendar to mark down all exercises (in my calendar, I use different initials for each sport)

13 - **Celebrate / share** all small achievements in the office (bragging allowed!)

14 - **Go shopping**, from time to time, for new sport equipment, new sports clothing, gadgets, applications etc.

15 - Have **motivational quotes scattered around your house** / office / laptop (here are two quotes that I have at home: **"Let's Go Champ"** from Boxing champion, Shannon Briggs and **"Mental Override"** thanks to tip of the author, Aubrey Markus!)

16 - On social media, **follow your great sporting heroes** (I follow: Cristiano Ronaldo , Notorious MacGregor ; David Goggins; Jocko Willink; Kilian Jornet; Lucy Charles-Barclay, Lionel Sanders and many more)

17 - Thinking about **medium/Long term Rewards**

> Start, Not Tomorrow, Now!!

Hal Elrod, writer of the book, "**Miracle Morning"** describes how he started with some short morning runs (the first time he went for a run he didn't even have running shoes and ran with basketball shoes) and how those runs became the trigger for a giant leap into a life filled with joy.

Hal Elrod built a powerful morning routine, shared it in his book, and it quickly became a life-changing routine for thousands of people around the world.

It only takes about 30 minutes to 1 hour, and has 6 steps:

SAVERS: Silence (Breathe),
Affirmations (Encourage),
Visualization (Imagine),
Exercise (Move),
Reading (Learn),
Scribing (Journal)

It's a small book that everybody should read:
"**The Miracle Morning:** The Not-So-Obvious Secret Guaranteed to Transform Your Life (Before 8AM) " by Hal Elrod

> "A day without Running is like a day without eating"
>
> Haile Gebrselassie

#051

10. SELF-LOVE

WORK ON YOUR CONFIDENCE

What comes first -
self-confidence or success?
I don't know. Either. It's a
"chicken and egg" situation.

What I do know is that no one is born brimming with confidence, and that no one in history has ever lived super confident (unless you slept through your teenage years).
Even George Clooney can lack confidence from time to time. In fact he once said: "Anyone would be lying if they said they didn't get lonely at times."

The bottom line is that confidence has to be worked on daily basis!

My brother Antonio works daily on this to the point of hitting a poor golf shot and convincing himself it was good. Everyone's a winner here - we all have a laugh at how ridiculous that was, and it also keeps HIS spirits up too!

3 people who triumphed over their insecurities and changed the history of the world:
- Mahatma Gandhi: was timid and shy, easily frightened, and afraid of the dark.
- Albert Einstein: discreet and shy, also considered a slow learner, had dyslexia.
- Thomas Edison: His teacher felt he was intellectually disabled, and he went to school for only three months.

Below are some tricks to improve daily CONFIDENCE:
Talk to yourself in a positive way. The head is the master of the body.
No one has ever scored a penalty saying to themselves: "I will fail, I will fail".
Also, it's not a great idea going to a posh nightclub in town, talking to the most beautiful human being in the place and saying to yourself: "I'm a loser, I'm a loser, I'm a loser".
I think you get it!

Even when you don't feel confident, **maintain a confident posture**. "Fake it till you make it". It's proven - your body will send positive messages to the head and you will feel better.

> **"If you're presenting yourself with confidence, you can pull off pretty much anything"**
>
> Katy Perry

#053

»

Choose clothes that you feel confident. **"Dress for success"**. At work, in sport, in your social life. One of my sisters-in-law, when she has a special occasion and is not entirely confident, she wears the clothes she wore on the day my brother proposed to her.

In sports, almost all champions have amulets, kits, or clothing that reminds them of past successes and builds their confidence.

Tiger Woods won several golf tournaments when he wore the red shirt on the final day.

Treat your body well. **Do exercise and take care of your image** including hair, nails etc.

Smile + Smile + Smile. Keep smiling and you'll start a positive cycle. If you can't smile do something else that works - happy songs, comedy movies, dinner with a funny friend, reminiscing about matches that your football team won.

Meditate. Just 10 minutes a day is enough to not get irritated with most small annoying things (and you will never say again "why does this only happen to me").

Take a minute each day to **think about three good things in life** (be creative, small, big, important, less important – it doesn't matter)

Learn new things – a new hobby, read about different subjects

Focus on positive things and avoid comparisons with others.
It is worth remembering the story of a person who was happy because he found €20 on the floor, but suddenly became very upset when he learned that his two friends had found €50 each.

"I AM THE GREATEST, I SAID THAT EVEN BEFORE I KNEW I WAS"

Muhammad Ali

11. REDUCE SOCIAL MEDIA

DISCONNECT TO CONNECT

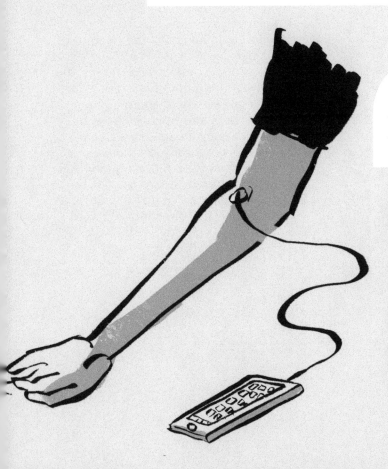

> **Impulsive web browsing and television watching is a disease of today's society.**

Zdravko Cvijetić Founder Of Zero To Skill

#055

#056

Here is another chapter that I personally still have room for improvement on. At home I have written on one of the walls: "SOCIAL MEDIA DETOX" - just a reminder to help me in the hard battle I fight on a daily basis.

It's sad to think that the first and last thing we see, and touch, every day is our mobile phone. It's even more depressing if we count the number of times per day that we WASTE checking the lives of others, instead of enjoying and investing in our own lives!

Even when we are at an amazing concert, sat just a few metres away from our favourite artist, we decide to see the show through the very small screen of our mobile phone to shoot and take pictures (to post on social media, the classic "in your face" #MyLifeIsBetterThanYours)

WHEN THE PHONE WAS TIED WITH WIRE, HUMANS WERE FREE!

Aravind K R

2 Nice rules that will make socializing more fulfilling:

- Rule for dinner - whoever touches the mobile phone, has to drink a full glass wine/beer!
(If you do not find the person in front of you interesting – don't blame them. Maybe you didn't ask the right question! You're the one who isn't interested)

- At home with my family, we take pictures of who is on the phone and put them on the family's WhatsApp group chat – a sort of the "Hall of Shame"!
This game improved so much that we started to enjoy it more, talk more, laugh more....

Some tricks that work for me:
- Have no colours on the screen of your mobile phone. Most of the time, my screen is just black and white (you can change this in your settings)

- Start wearing a wristwatch again (it will reduce the amount of time you look at a mobile)

- During dinners/ lunches / meetings, remove notifications / sound / turn the screen down

- Don't take your mobile phone into the bedroom (a good friend tells me that in bed he only does 2 things 😊)

- Ask somebody to bully you - someone who makes you feel bad whenever you use it.

A book that helped me here was:
How to Break Up with Your Phone - Catherine Price

The internet and social media have tools with unbelievable power, therefore becoming a source of inspiration or destruction. This 10 year old kid I know went to Google and searched:
"Best Football Player of 4th grade class C at school located in neighbourhood

⟩⟩ one escapes our Hall of Shame. My father is also addicted to his mobile phone
y father with my brother António, sister Maria and nephew Francisco)

XXXX" Their parents where very proud telling me that they found that search in the browser history. But one year later they found something a bit different in that browser history of the same kid. He was searching for one word only:
"Tits"

Use social media to expand your mind, to grow! If you follow interesting pages on social media and do plenty of likes in those pages, they will appear on your wall many times. I like to follow these:
https://www.facebook.com/lifehackorg/
https://www.facebook.com/thriveglbl/
https://www.facebook.com/HigherPerspective/
https://www.facebook.com/Addicted2SuccessDotCom/
https://www.facebook.com/BigThinkdotcom/
https://www.facebook.com/anthonyrobbinsinspiration/
https://www.facebook.com/EntMagazine/
https://www.facebook.com/forbes/
https://www.facebook.com/HBR/
(also available in all other Social media channels)

In an article from Fast Company (Feb,2018) called **"Even Instagram thinks you´re spending too much time on Instagram"** we are told about two new features; the notice "You´re All Caught Up" , when you´ve seen all and it´s time to live your real life, and the feature "Do Not Disturb". Even Instagram and Facebook know we are all spending too much time on their channels!!
The article finishes saying: **"in 2018 tec is selling mindfulness, not addiction."**

MANY OF US WILL NEVER ACHIEVE OUR GOALS, WILL NEVER REALISE OUR DREAMS, BECAUSE OF OUR MOBILE PHONE.

11. REDUCE SOCIAL MEDI

Not yet totally convinced?
Steve Jobs and Bill Gates, the world's biggest technology visionaries, founders of Apple and Microsoft, KNOW THE RISKS WELL!

Bill Gates, didn't let his kids get mobile phones until they turned 14!
Bill Gates also implemented a maximum cap on screen time to his daughter.
Steve Jobs forbid his kids from using the newly-released iPad. and also said: "We limit how much technology our kids use at home,"

From an article by The Guardian (23rd Jan 2018)
"'Never get high on your own supply' - why social media bosses don't use social media.

Developers of platforms such as Facebook have admitted that they were designed to be addictive.
'Social media executives are following the rules of pushers and dealers everywhere.'
https://www.theguardian.com/media/2018/jan/23/never-get-high-on-your-own-supply-why-social-media-bosses-dont-use-social-media

#059

12. USE THE 80-20 RULE

Churchill

Vilfredo Pareto was a 19th century thinker who concluded that 20% of the population owned 80% of the properties. He managed to identify numerous similar correlations.

It was only 2 centuries later I was able to understand the Pareto principle, with the book **"The 80/20 Principle"** by Richard Koch.
That's the recipe for achieving more results with less effort.
Basically about 20% of the inputs generate approximately 80% of the outputs.

I HAVE ACHIEVED MANY
THINGS BECAUSE I
DO NOT CONSUME MY
ENERGY IN VAIN.
I DO NOT STAND IF I CAN
SIT AND I DO NOT SIT IF I
CAN LIE DOWN

Winston Churchill

#061

The formula applies to an endless number of variables and became a golden rule and mindset of efficient people.

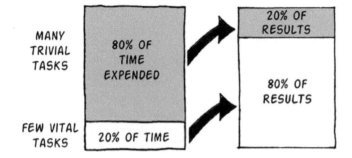

80/20 Mindset Examples:

- A small part of my time is responsible for the largest part of my income. I will identify these periods, give them more consistency and deliberately allocate the unprofitable time to leisure activities.

- Do customer analysis and understand that a small slice of my customers generate the biggest bulk of the results. I can give more exclusive attention to the 20% that are valuable, and dismiss some of the 80% that takes too much time without much profit.

- There is a minority, 20%, of the people who give us 80% of the joys! Focus on those people and start often giving up on toxic people. Remember what Jim Rohn said:

"You are the average of the five people you spend the most time with."

There are HUGE Differences between busy and productive people!
Are you keeping yourself busy to hide from the important stuff ?

DON'T BE A BUSY FOOL!

Focus on the " few vital tasks" that will really make a difference in your life!

Use 80/20 mindset to prioritise the important aspects of your life.
Use the 80/20 Mindset to focus on what can really make a difference in your life! It's a great investment to take some time to really think about this and start using the 80/20 Rule!

One of the most successful investors in history Ray Dalio (founder of the world's biggest hedge fund firm, Bridgewater Associates) has that mindset well sorted:
"you can have anything you want in life but you can't have everything you want"

"Don't let yourself be paralyzed by all the choices." -> PRIORITISE

13. MANAGE YOUR TIME

If all goes OK we are expected to live well into our 80s.....or 30,000 days. The countdown is ON! Each day you lose is never recovered!

> **Remembering that i'll be dead soon is the most important tool I've ever encountered to help me make big choices in life**
>
> Steve Jobs

A close friend is a hotel general manager – a full time job in a demanding industry. Married with 2 kids, he weighed more than 100 kgs (220 pounds)!
3 years later: 70 Kg (154 pounds), 2x IronMan (qualified for Kona finals in Hawaii) while maintaining the standard as hotel professional and a family man.

NO EXCUSES!

Stuff that Worked:
Cutting TV time; shorter lunch times; delegate in a better way;
Running while your wife and son are enjoying an easy bike ride (you can still talk or even pretend you are listening ☺)
Cycling with your indoor bike while you help you son with his homework.
Taking deep breaths in the car (10 mins) on the way to work, or listen to audiobooks

A romantic trip the day before the race (relax)
A couple of massages the day after the race
"Lack of time is lack of priorities"

TIME (from the book "Essentialism" - Greg Mckeown)
Time is the most precious asset in the world.
The quote **"Time is money"** is not a good one because time is worth more than money.
If today I didn't win x Euros, tomorrow I might win 3x more.
It is not the same case when we lose time...

PROTECT YOUR TIME FIERCELY!
Everyone wants your time! Your boss, your girlfriend or boyfriend, your friends, family, acquaintances.....even your dog (the only one who can't complain much).
Please remember:

IF YOU DON'T MAKE YOUR AGENDA, SOMEONE WILL DO IT FOR YOU!

The way to protect **your time** is to learn to say NO!!
"Learn the slow yes and the fast no!"
Practice the art of saying NO! It gets easier and will save you LOTS of time.
Remember that when you say **"NO"** you

might lose popularity (momentarily), but it will ultimately garner respect. Tim Ferriss (entrepreneur, author, and podcaster) talks about his decision method for accepting, or not, a commitment:

HELL YEAHHH or No!

In a study done with terminally ill people, most of whom had less than 12 weeks to live,
their biggest regret was:
"I wish I had the courage to live a true life for me, and not the life that others expected from me!"

 garyvee

OH...YOU HAVE TIME...YOU JUST PICKED SOMETHING ELSE.

YOU ARE YOUR CALENDAR!

We are what we do repeatedly.
If you continue making that same routine **work-home-work**, you won't have any good stories to tell your grandchildren.
Personally, I always had great difficulties in saying NO and, many times, I felt that I was always running, from one place to another, to keep other people happy, or take part in some activity or social occasion that, deep down, I didn't even like.
That was until I discovered a trick! (drum roll, please)
BLOCKING TIMES IN YOUR DIARY, with nothing – JUST TIME FOR ME!!
Just do your schedule for next week before your mother-in-law starts calling you with some ideas for the weekend!
If someone checks out your diary, you can even put fictitious commitments like: **"Medical appointment"** or **"Statistical data analysis"** or **"Conference Call with CEO"** ☺
Don't feel bad, **when it comes to protecting your time**, it's Just like UFC (*), **there's NO RULES!!**
(*)Ultimate Fighting Championship

Some ideas:
• Book 4 dates (and tickets) for great gigs during the year
• Block 1 hour per day for yourself (see Miracle Morning - Hal Elrod).
• Arrive 30 minutes early to work , and leave work 30 minutes before to make time for a walk or swim.

#066

>>

Block the dates for the carnival in Brazil, Oktoberfest or St. Patrick's Day

Think of the things that really make you happy and the achievements or events you wouldn't forget in a hurry.
Think about your priorities: Family, Physical, Mental, Work.
Think about your schedule in the last 2 months, are you any getting closer?

Some points that I'm working on (but that I still suck at)

Answering less phone calls (please send a text message)
Resisting the temptation to reply immediately to emails or messages
Refusing meetings

When we say that famous line: "I don't have time" we know we are lying to ourselves. The day has 24 hours and as the famous entrepreneur Gary Vaynerchuk says:

"Show me your schedule, YOU WILL GET EXPOSED!"

"if you don't fill your day with high priority items, others will fill your day with low priority items"
– the 1% rule – Tommy Baker

24 HOURS of a typical day:
- 7 hours sleep
- 8 hours work
- 3 hours meals
- 2 hours transport
- 2 hours household chores
= 22 Hours!!

2 hours left ⟶ Wasting time on social Media, watching TV instead of working on your Goals or dreams or hobbies.
- See your breakdown of hours for a typical day and you will come to the same conclusion.
- **1 hour a day of focus would be enough to be INCREDIBLE in whatever you want!**
(1 hour free time, in case you come up with the excuse that you need to help your children with homework)

⟶ When we start thinking about minutes instead of hours, we move to another level with even more focus and less waste!

In a great excerpt from the renowned FORBES magazine I read:

"Highly successful people know that there are 1,440 minutes in every day and there is nothing more valuable than time. Money can be lost and made again, but time spent can never be reclaimed.
As legendary Olympic gymnast Shannon Miller told me,
"To this day, I keep a schedule that is almost minute by minute."
You must master your minutes to master your life."

**"You don't have to be the victim of your environment.
You can also be the architect of it."**

James Clear

#067

14. EMBRACE THE 4 AGREEMENTS

BY DON MIGUEL RUIZ

Listed as one of the Watkins 100 Most Spiritually
Influential Living People
- New York Times **Bestseller** + than **7 years**.
"A Practical Guide to Personal Freedom"

This book is a short (and wonderful) manual
for a better and less complicated life.
There are 4 simple rules - but they must be
practiced daily.
I have these 4 rules printed, in Big letters, in
the office and at home.

1 - Be impeccable with your word!

Use the power of your word in the direction of truth and love -Avoid using the word to speak against yourself or gossip about others

100 times easier on a theoretical level but we should at least try to improve. I have to admit that it is fun to listen to some gossip but, we also know, when we gossip we don't gain huge respect from whoever is listening ...

"Don't be fooled... if they gossip to you, they'll gossip about you."

Steve Maraboli

The word has a huge power, for good and bad, so we have to use it better! It can save us from humiliation and creates a positive aura around us. Even in relation to ourselves, the word is VERY powerful. We spend our lives self-criticising

THINK BEFORE YOU SPEAK, WORDS CAN HURT AND ONCE IT'S BEEN SAID, YOU CAN NEVER TAKE IT BACK.

ourselves and this negatively affects our self-esteem and performance. If a stranger told you 10% of the negative things you say to yourself, you would probably punch him (or, at least, think about it). We have to speak to ourselves in a very positive way! (but not out loud, OK?)

Speaking of punching, the great Muhammed Ali was a master at using the word as an ally for self-belief – crucial to all his achievements!

#069

2 - Don't take it personally!

- Nothing others do is because of you!
- What others say or do is a projection of their own reality or dream.

I remember occasions when I achieved a sales record and my boss didn't congratulate me, maybe even adding something like:
"Hey, I'm worried about sales for the next quarter!! Do something"

I hated that situation because I thought people were just not giving me credit for my big effort!

Today, I am learning "not to take it personally". Whenever that happens I try to focus on the message, simply, that the company needs more sales and that my boss does not have the time to choose perfect words like Winston Churchill to motivate his troops!
Practicing **"Don't take it personally"** made me face irritating situations with more ease, because the reason behind attitudes or words chosen by others is rarely because of something we have done.
(Some things do not change though. Us Portuguese, can quite easily lose the plot in traffic jams! 😊)

ANNOUNCING "I'M OFFENDED" IS BASICALLY TELLING THE WORLD YOU CAN'T CONTROL YOUR OWN EMOTIONS, SO EVERYONE ELSE SHOULD DO IT FOR YOU.

" I am here today to cross the swamp, not to fight all the alligators.

from The Art of Possibility by Rosamund and Benjamin Zander

14. EMBRACE THE

3 - Don't Make Assumptions

- Find the courage to ask questions and express what you really want.
- Communicate with others as clearly as you can to avoid misunderstandings, sadness and drama.

We tend to assume that a colleague who doesn't say "Good Morning" doesn't like us.
But then maybe if you make conversation you'll find out that she was stuck in horrible traffic on the way to work, hates driving and even thinks you are the "Brad Pitt" of your office.

How many times do we jump to conclusions only to find our later that we are miles away from what was actually going on!

#071

GREEMENTS

4 – Always do your best!

- Under any circumstance, simply do your best, and you will avoid self-judgment, self-abuse, and regret.

Even on days when we are not a 100%, if we do the best we can we will still be at peace with ourselves, even if we do not reach our goals.
The night before my 1st marathon, Berlin 2015, I slept surprisingly well despite having a great challenge ahead of me. That night I felt peaceful because I already finished a very tough training program for 4 consecutive months. Whatever happened, good or bad, I would easily deal with it!

Jesé Rodríguez: "I remember the first time I went to Real Madrid's training ground. I got there two hours earlier to impress my coaches but when I got there I saw Cristiano Ronaldo already training"

15. YOU ARE IN SALES

(become a Master)

Whether you like it or not, YOU work in sales!
Whatever job you have, you are in the sales business.
In life, and at home, benefits are even bigger if you become a more effective persuader.
Admit it, and start to become an expert at it!!

EVEN A DOCTOR WHO
IS TECHNICALLY GIFTED
– IF HE DOESN'T PORTRAY
HIMSELF AS BEING
TRUSTWORTHY AND KIND,
ODDS ARE, HE WON'T HAVE
MANY PATIENTS

I´ve read many books about sales and attended many seminars about different sales techniques.
To make your life easy, I will tell you now the best advice!
The one advice that will make your "sales job" easy! (REALLY??? yes, trust me!)

"FIND SOMETHING TO LIKE ABOUT THE PERSON IN FRONT OF YOU!"

It can be anything!
Just Search, **Ask questions & Listen carefully!** You will be surprised:
You both have a dog, support the same football team, have kids same age, love the beach, hate traffic!
(use this but be careful not to fall in love with everybody)

I DON'T LIKE THAT MAN. I MUST GET TO KNOW HIM BETTER.

Abraham Lincoln

When you start liking the person in front of you, then the rest of the sales technique becomes just a piece of cake!
You will become a genius for **"INSTANT INTIMACY"** because:

You will **SMILE easily** (even if it's not that funny)
Make **eye contact** without any effort (but don't be a psycho, please)
You will enjoy **complimenting** them
You will use their **FIRST NAME** ("the sweetest and most important sound in any language")
You will **lighten up**, passing on good vibes (humour is just disarming)
Offer them a **Hot Drink**
You will **Mirror** the other person naturally
Touch (careful here)
You will **find** more **common ground**
*(Find more in the BOOK: **The Good Psychopath's Guide to Success** by Andy McNab and Kevin Dutton)*

Studies Show:
*If asking a favour, start with someone's **NAME**, they are much more likely to help!*

*Waitresses, who **TOUCH** clients on the arm earn considerably more tips!*

#075

#076

By now the "prospect", or whoever you want to influence, already likes you!
He might forget about the competition and will remember you.
Work on these 5 topics to become the Cristiano Ronaldo of sales:
- **Clarity & keep it short** (nowadays the "elevator pitch" has become too long)
- **What's in it for him?** (speak in their language, understand their goals)
- **Adopt an attitude of "service"**
- **Believe in your value** (and the value of the product)
- **Patience** (watch out, too much persistence is a turn-off)
And please, please, **No HARD selling!!**

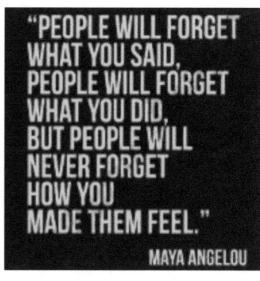

"PEOPLE WILL FORGET WHAT YOU SAID, PEOPLE WILL FORGET WHAT YOU DID, BUT PEOPLE WILL NEVER FORGET HOW YOU MADE THEM FEEL."

MAYA ANGELOU

If you are still not sure about this, please listen to Seth Godin (writer of 18 bestsellers and described in Forbes magazine as the "King of Marketing")

"There's no such thing as a born salesperson.
What there are... are people with empathy and learned charisma who choose to work hard. ... you will have a skill for life."

Seth's BLOG, on August 25th , 2018
https://seths.blog/2018/08/the-born-salesperson/

ARNOLD SCHWARZENEGGER WALKING THROUGH MUNICH IN SWIMMING TRUNKS IN ORDER DO PROMOTE HIS OWN GYM (1969)

16. PRACTICE GRATITUDE

"I NEVER MET A BITTER
PERSON WHO WAS
THANKFUL.
OR A THANKFUL PERSON
WHO WAS BITTER."

Nick Vujicic

#077

Gratitude is a source of happiness.
In Salvador, Brazil, I spoke to people who live in great poverty but who radiated happiness. They were always smiling, always dancing, thankful for the life they had, thankful for their family and friends.

Gratitude has to be practiced daily.
Some points to think and thank daily:
- **Having a home**
- **The taste of the food (eating more slowly helps)**
- **Clean clothes**
- **Friends**
- **Family**

Pay special attention to the little things we take for granted every day!

Inspired by the Book **"CALM: Calm the Mind. Change the World"** by Michael Acton Smith

Do this every day...... in the car, in the sauna, when you wake up, before you go to sleep.
Think about:
3 best things of the day + 3 things I'm grateful for + 1 thing that made me calm.

These things can be big and important things, but also the most simple and stupid things!

Some examples I normally think of: (you're allowed to copy these!)

3 best things of the day:
Great music I heard in the car, a great dessert, a funny joke that I said in the office (this happens to me a lot! Hahah), lunch with my nephews, beer with friends, giving or receiving advice, a silly joke I heard on the phone, I won at padel tennis and irritated friends after with an "in your face", asking my nieces little questions, noticing that the girls in the bar were dazzled staring at me (hahahhaah), offering a book to a friend, letting my mum know that she has food in her teeth.

3 things I'm Grateful for:
my apartment, having a job, friendly colleagues, the opportunity to travel, parents, friends, nephews, good meals, health, being able to run and do sports, friend's messages, the commitment of my teammates, being (without any doubt) the most handsome of all my brothers 😊

1 thing that made me Calm:
Sunbathing, enjoying the sauna in silence, listening to calm music, not looking at a mobile phone during a meal, breathing while counting slowly from fifty to zero, skipping programs to have spare time with nothing booked, running very early, listening to the sea, swimming with dolphins during sunset (hahaahhaha)

> **"Be thankful for what you have; you'll end up having more. If you concentrate on what you don't have, you will never, ever have enough."**

Oprah Winfrey

Also, on the subject of gratitude, it's VERY Difficult to actually say these nice things to the people that are in our lives every day.

I heard that once there was a Fin who loved his wife SO MUCH the he almost told her!! Let's work on this so we don't become like this guy!

I do not want to be pessimistic (and this is just another reminder), but it seems to me that in the ultra-fast modern world of social media, e-mails etc. the tendency is to forget to stop for a couple of minutes - to be thankful for so many blessings.

I see this a lot with my nephews and it really makes me laugh. Recently I texted my two nieces with a great video about surfing with some incredible waves (both of them are athletes, so I thought it could be inspirational).

The answer I was EXPECTING: - Hello Uncle, wonderful video, thank you, I miss you Uncle! Kisses.

The reality was slightly different 😊:

One replied: Uncle, I already have seen this video before!

The other, didn't even reply!

(hahahahah)

If that's not enough you can read a Forbes article (by Amy Morin- Mental strength trainer and international bestselling mental strength author)

7 SCIENTIFICALLY PROVEN BENEFITS OF GRATITUDE

1. **Gratitude opens the door to more relationships.**
2. **Gratitude improves physical health.**
3. **Gratitude improves psychological health.**
4. **Gratitude enhances empathy and reduces aggression.**
5. **Grateful people sleep better.**
6. **Gratitude improves self-esteem.**
7. **Gratitude increases mental strength.**

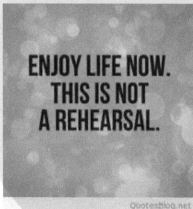

ENJOY LIFE NOW. THIS IS NOT A REHEARSAL.

QuotesBlog.net

17. DISCOVER NEW HOBBIES

(Never too late)

Grandma Moses (1860 –1961) began painting at the age of 78!
One of her painting was sold for US $1.2 million!

The right time is created by the power of a bold decision

Tommy Baker (The 1% Rule)

Trying new hobbies boosts your work performance, makes you smarter and, even more important , it's FUN!!!!

In a nice article (*) in LifeHack website by Nabin Paudyal (Co-Founder, Siplikan Media Group)
Taking Up These 10 Hobbies Will Make You Smarter

1. Play a musical instrument.
2. Read voraciously.
3. Meditate regularly.
4. Work out your brain. (sudoku, puzzles, board games, riddles, etc)
5. Exercise often.
6. Learn a new language.
7. Write your feelings down.
8. Travel to new places.
9. Cook different kinds of meals.
10. Participate in sport actively.
(*) http://www .lifehack.org/310690/taking-these-10-hobbies-will-make-you-smarter

No wonder that the majority of successful people, from the present and the past, have developed and engaged in hobbies, some even quite unexpected:
- **Warren Buffet** (One of the world's most successful investors): Ukulele
- **Richard Branson** (Business magnate): Kite Surf and Chess

- **Jack Dorsey** (Twitter): Hiking
- **Marissa Mayer** (Yahoo): Cook Cup Cakes
- **David Salomon** (Goldman Sachs): DJ
- **Agatha Christie** (world's best-selling author of all time): Archeology
- **Sylvia Plath** (Poet): Bee keeping
- **Alice Cooper** (legendary hard rock & metal musician): Golf
- **Mark Twain** (author of books like "Adventures of Tom Sawyer") Amateur inventor
- **Ernest Hemingway** (Writer & Pulitzer Prize winner): Sailing and Fishing
- **Orville & Wilbur Wright** (these brothers invented the aeroplane): they loved bicycles, raced them, collected them!

3 Former Presidents of United States, below, also taking hobbies seriously:
- **Teddy Roosevelt:** hunting, boxing, horse riding, hiking, reading, writing and scouting
- **Thomas Jefferson:** chess, writing, playing the violin, architecture, archaeology, cooking and designing libraries.
- **Franklin D. Roosevelt**, once said, *"I owe my life to my hobbies — especially stamp collecting."*

#082

→ **Some people, close to me, who followed interesting paths taking new hobbies:**

A co-worker, he is an engineer, has a daughter who does triathlon, and took the opportunity to start taking pictures of his daughter during competitions and making short videos of those events.

My sister-in-law, she was a pathological anatomy technician at the hospital, and started painting as a hobby at 35 years old. She felt so enthusiastic about it that, after a few years, it became her new profession with a salary well above her old job.

A good friend who was addicted to rugby and jiu-jitsu and learned recently to play the piano and absolutely loves it now (he did try keep this hobby as a secret, for fear that his manhood would be hurt, but , fortunately, sometimes, the word gets out! 😊)

Even with the strangest hobby in the world, MAGIC happens:

- **Gardening:** Craig Jenkings-Sutton started gardening in 2003 as a hobby but in 2011 this "little enjoyment" was already selling $ 1.2 million.
(source. Entreperneur.com)

- **Making drawings on the back of business cards:** Hugh MacLeod, tired of the corporate world, to distract himself, he liked to make drawings on the back of business cards when taking breaks from work at his local café. He opened Gapingvoid.com blog to expose "recreations" that transformed his life. His book **"Ignore Everybody"** made the list of best sellers in the Wall Street Journal.

- **Eating Hot Dogs:** the Japanese, Takeru Kobayashi, investigated and searched carefully for a new technique to eat hot dogs as fast as he could. In 2001, he ate 50 Hot Dogs in 12 minutes (the old record was 25) during the famous "Nathan´s Hot Dog Eating Contest"

(no no, this is
not Karate Kid again,
this is Takeru Kobayashi,
himself, our Hot Dog eating
champion!!)

It's never too late:

RAY KROC

Ray Kroc: Started **Mcdonalds** at 52

HENRY FORD

Henry Ford: Started **FORD** at 40

HARLAND SANDLERS

Harland Sandlers: started **KFC** at 65

SAM WALTON

Sam Walton: started **Walmart** at 44

> "If you want something you've never had You must be willing to do something you've never done."
>
> Thomas Jefferson

@ Palmares Golf, Algarve, in 2010 , with my twin brother and Robert Trent Jones's Team. Robert Trent Jones Jr, in green, one of the best golf architects in the world, loves to write poems as a hobby to relax and inspire him.

#083

18. FIND SOMETHING FUNNY EVERYDAY

A DAY WITHOUT LAUGHTER IS A DAY WASTED

Charlie Chaplin

More and more studies indicate that laughing can reduce stress, improve immune system, lower blood pressure, boost mood , reduce depression and help you live longer!

Richard Wiseman, in his Book, Quirkology: How We Discover the Big Truths in Small Things, reveals an interesting study of James Rotton (psychologist at Florida International University) who examined the effects of what watching different kinds of films (serious or funny) had on hospital patients recovering from orthopedic surgery.

The discovery was that patients who were watching funny films used about 60 percent fewer pain-relieving drugs than those looking at the serious movies.

Please note, I am not asking you be funny.
One of my brothers, Antonio, has a routine to read a joke every day. After 2 years, he is still not funny (there are no miracles) but it gives him a great boost in the morning and he is enjoying it a lot!!
Just start cultivating the ability to put some perspective and find funny stuff in your day to day life.

dudewithsign @ Instagram (Seth has 7 Million followers and counting)

19. MAKE AN EFFORT TO LOOK BETTER

YOU CANNOT
CLIMB THE LADDER
OF SUCCESS
DRESSED IN THE
COSTUME OF
FAILURE

Zig Ziglar

Don't worry, this is not going to be the part where I become a "fashion advisor".
I am the last person in the world who can give advice or beauty tips.
About 95% of my shirts are the same colour - white - and I also wear the same shoes, every day, black moccasins (but NEVER with trinkets!!), just to make sure I don't make silly mistakes.

-What we all know, like it or not, is that **what we choose to wear has an effect on us and also on other people.**
Put on boxing gloves for a fight.
Put on the football boots before running onto the pitch
Put on make-up before going on stage
Put on a helmet plus leather jacket before motorcycle ride
What you choose to use is a statement of what you are going to do and how you see yourself.
If you are going to the office, why not make an extra effort to look good?

If you are going to have a drink, make an effort! A little something extra to look a bit better!
Adding that extra bit of style to your day won't hurt anybody.
(just be careful not to break anybody's hearts!)
Make the effort and soon you will feel more confident, improve your self-esteem, put yourself in a good mood, and as a consequence others will be more friendly to you, starting a positive vicious circle!!

Dress to impress & Dress for success

GO OUT ALL DAY LOOKING GREAT AND I SEE NO ONE! BUT IF I WALK OUT FOR 5 MINUTES LOOKING LIKE SHIT, SUDDENLY IT'S LIKE A F***ING REUNION.

#087

20. BELIEVE IN YOURSELF

"WHETHER YOU THINK YOU CAN OR CAN'T, YOU ARE RIGHT"

Henry Ford

"If you're searching for that one person that will change your life, take a look in the mirror."

OK, I have to believe me, I get it. But how?

If you say twenty times the words "I will make a good speech" or "I will be brilliant at the meeting" or "I will make a great presentation" it will make no difference unless you've done your preparation or homework.

Those big champions' inner belief and confidence is made up of daily work with small daily victories.

Small accumulated victories start enhancing your confidence, pave the way to bigger challenges and soon even greater victories start materializing naturally.

The legendary Navy SEAL, Admiral William McRaven, with a military career spanning 37 years, responsible for the capture of Bin Laden, in a graduation speech for an American university said: *"If you want to change the world, **start off by making your bed**. If you make your bed every morning, you will have accomplished the first task of the day. It will give you a small sense of pride, and it will encourage you to do another task, and another, and another. By the end of the day, that one task completed will have turned into many tasks completed. Making your bed will also reinforce the fact that little things in life matter. If you can't do the little things right, you'll never be able to do the big things right. If, by chance, you have a miserable day, you will come home to a bed that's made. That you made. And a made bed gives you encouragement that tomorrow will be better."*

Start by getting used to getting things done! The best way to believe in yourself is through routine, which in turn allows us to get used to believing in ourselves.

Those small and consistent daily achievements are the ones that can make us successful people.

1999: Jeff Bezos @ his office ☺

BELIEVE IN YOURSELF

> "The biggest difference I've noticed between successful people and unsuccessful people isn't intelligence or opportunity or resources. It's the belief that they can make their goals happen."

James Clear

All top performers in the world, know well

THE INCREDIBLE POWER OF VISUALIZING SUCCESS & GOALS

- Golf legend, **Tiger Woods**, in his routine visualization exercise, closes his eyes and imagines every single shot, one by one, from the first to the very last putt on the 18th Hole.
- The famous **creator of Dilbert, Scott Adams**, visualized and wrote his dreams fifteen times in a row, every single day!
- The early days of **actor Jim Carey** were difficult. He worked as a janitor, lived in a van and fought dyslexia. In 1990 he wrote a cheque to himself, for USD 10 million to be cashed in 1995, and he kept it in his wallet!
Just before Thanksgiving 1995 he got the new the news we would receive USD 10 million for the movie "Dumb and Dumber"!

A personal achievement which reminds me how visualising goals really can work incredibly well was when I did my first (and only) IronMan triathlon. It was a seven month training program. Two months before the end, I started to believe it might be possible to finish all 226Kms (140 miles) of the IronMan in under ten hours. So I started visualising that target during every training session while swimming, running and on the bike. When the BIG day came the result was **9h59m35s**. (I still had 24 seconds to do some push-ups 😊)

How to improve your visualisation technique:
Write down your goals in a very visible place
Talk to yourself, repeat & repeat (It´s OK, we are all a bit crazy anyway!)
Imagine you as the hero!
Include as many details possible
Visualise short-term and long-term goals

2 Tigers, side by side, hahahah!
(Left)Tiger Woods, winning the US Open, in 2000, by 15 shots
It remains the most dominating performance and victory in any major championship.
(Right) Me, after surviving the swim leg, IronMan @ Victoria-Gasteiz, 14th July 2018

SOMETIMES THE THING THAT IS HOLDING YOU BACK... IS ALL IN YOUR HEAD

"It's the repetition of affirmations that leads to belief. And once that belief becomes a deep conviction, things begin to happen."

Muhammad Ali

"No one knows enough to be a pessimist"

Wayne Dyer

#091

21. FEED FRIENDSHIP

Shipwrecked, an average man and Claudia Schiffer are the only survivors on a desert island. In the face of so much loneliness, they became a couple. The man was glowing with happiness!!! After two weeks, Claudia Schiffer starts to notice that the man was becoming sad, more and more each day. So she said she was ready to do everything he wanted just to make him happy again! So the man asked her to meet him for dinner at the end of the day, but dressed as a man and looking like a Man. When she finally appeared, for dinner, the two of them sat down and so the man said energetically with a giant smile to his "friend":
"Do you know who I've been sleeping with the last 2 weeks???

A Michigan State University study by psychology professor William Chopik suggests that **friends can bring you more happiness and health than your family members.**
"Friends are a conscious choice. Family relationships can be serious, negative and monotonous. " (the in-laws, play a HUGE part here, hahah)

Family cannot replace friends. (not even friends replace family, of course).
Make a conscious effort to nurture important friendships. You can use all possible alibis to be together or connect:
football, birthdays, kids parties, texting jokes, playing sports together etc.

If you happen to see a friend on the street, don't say things you don't mean......
"Let's go for lunch or dinner sometime"
We all know that this lunch or dinner will NEVER happen.
The only way to really make it happen is to agree, right there and then, an exact day and block that time!

FRIENDS
ARE LIKE
THERAPISTS
THAT YOU
CAN DRINK
WITH

#093

22. PRACTICE SELF-COMPASSION

(Inspired by Emma Seppala's Book "The Happiness Track")

We are addicted to harsh and destructive self-criticism, and we even think that it helps us to be a little better prepared for this screwed up world. Emma Seppala's research shows that this is the wrong way round! Scientific data - supported by neuroscience and psychology studies - shows that the usual self-criticism makes us weaker when we fail, and makes us more emotional and difficult to assimilate lessons from these events. (in short, it just makes us dull and lonely).

Does this mean long live self-flattery and self-admiration even at times of personal failures and defeats? Calm down, guys, there must be a kind of break-event point!
The alternative to self-Criticism is self-compassion.
Self-compassion is treating ourselves as a friend would treat us.
We´ve mentioned it before, what would we think of a friend if he spoke to us with the same cruelty we speak to ourselves.
What we expect from a friend is that he understands the situation within the given context, in a calmer way and with a long-term perspective.

→ **Is this You?**

If we can be a little more compassionate with ourselves, research shows that we will be stronger, more resilient and more successful!

Musicians Kurt Cobain and DJ Avicii - both with incredible worldwide success - entered a negative spiral of self-destruction that led to suicide.

"If you want to change your life, figure out, how your worst day was your best day"

Tony Robbins

#095

23. POSITIVITY

AT A JOB INTERVIEW...

EMPLOYER: "WHAT ARE YOUR STRENGTHS?"

CANDIDATE: "I AM AN OPTIMIST & A
            POSITIVE THINKER"

EMPLOYER: "CAN YOU GIVE ME AN EXAMPLE?"

CANDIDATE: "YES... WHEN DO I START?"

There was never a successful entrepreneur who was not optimistic, and there was never a champion in any sport who was pessimistic. (although some can bluff pretending to be negative)
In 1963, just before the famous **"I have a dream"** speech, Martin Luther King was NOT thinking:

"Today I don't feel like giving a speech, I'm a very boring person"

It's also almost Impossible to score a decisive penalty to win the World Cup thinking:

"I am a loser, I always fail!"

Mother Teresa Calcutta made a difference in thousands and thousands of lives because, even in the midst of extreme poverty, she always managed to find a positive angle.

If we want to succeed, we have to work daily to be more positive even when faced with unexpected adversity.
The path of negativity is destructive.
It never triumphs and it can be a bottomless pit.
It is worth remembering the glass full/empty cliché.
If we get used to seeing the glass half empty, things can get worse:

"Some people come into your life as blessings. Others come into your life as lessons."

Mother Teresa

#097

24. EMBRACE DISCOMFORT

Just before all the best moments in life we feel some discomfort and fear. Successful people have become used to associate that discomfort, fear and anxiety with good things. They know that this is just the body sending signals that they are getting closer and closer to achieving something new, something important.
They know, above all, that it is time to move forward.

Sometimes before the Olympic Games or some other big sport event, we hear journalists asking the athletes:
- "Are you nervous?"
Usually the great champions, those who make history, always answer something like:
- "Nervous No, I am excited and eager for my moment to come."
Years later, when they have retired from sport, these great champions always say that what they miss most is to feel the typical anxiety before those great moments.
We have to get used to this and start associating the feeling "I am a bit nervous" to the positive things that are about to happen and just enjoy the moment.

Behind every fear is the person you want to be Greg Plitt

Feel The Fear And Do It Anyway Susan Jeffers

On a daily basis, if we have a routine of always doing what is just comfortable, we are condemned to failure. We will spend our days watching movies under a big thick blanket while eating popcorn and chocolate.
Growth is found when we face adversity, or when facing the unknown, or just wanting to go a little further. The fear of failure cannot outweigh the desire to win or reach our goals.
We often hear that **"adversity builds our character"** and also that **"adversity reveals character"**.
Both versions are true.
Every difficult moment we manage to overcome, we get stronger.
And, at the same time, each new difficult moment that lies ahead is an opportunity to show what we are made of!

David Goggins (retired United States Navy SEAL) , in his book "Can't Hurt Me: Master Your Mind and Defy the Odds" talks about the traumas of his childhood, he was often beaten by his father, he faced strong racism in school, etc. To David that became an impulse to become one of The Toughest Man Alive!!
David became an inspiration to millions of people, and with his mental strength became a ultramarathon runner, ultra-distance triathlete and world record holder for the most pull-ups in 24 hours.

#099

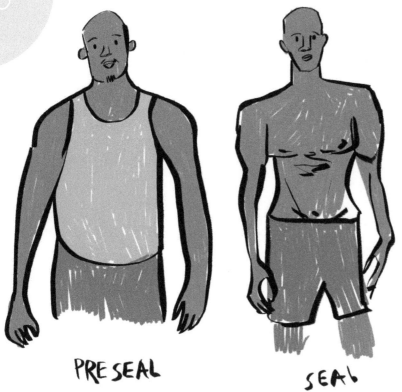

PRE SEAL

SEAL

"Allow Your Pain To Push You To Greatness."

Eric Thomas

"Do something that sucks every day of your life. That's how you grow. Embrace the suck."

David Goggins

If you are given everything without making any effort from your side, it's impossible to develop any type of muscle or mental resilience, and you w fail easily when you face the very first adversity.

So many people win millions on the lottery and very soon are left with nothing again.

So many spoiled kids who had everything they ever wished for, made zero effort, and later ruined family fortunes that took generations to buil

For people who had success, the adversities of the past are their greate: allies.

Adversity is seen almost as a blessing the winners.

Going to prison could be one of the worst times in a person's life...
4 Great figures in world history who wrote books while in prison:

- **Martin Luther King Jr.**
- **Miguel de Cervantes (Don Quixote)**
- **Nelson Mandela**
- **Oscar Wilde**

On a different note, several musicians transformed their sad love stories into the inspiration to write and compose songs that remained forever in history:

- **ABBA:** one of their most famous songs, **"The Winner Takes it all"**, sold, just in the pre-sale stage, **2 million copies**. This song was inspired by the painful separation between two of the four members of the band....who had to continue seeing each other every day for work.

- **Adele:** sold 17 million copies and made £ 25 million with the album she composed after her boyfriend abandoned her.

- **Alanis Morissette** - wrote the song "You Oughta Know" full of anger about a separation from an ex-boyfriend. That music that won "Best Rock song of the year" at the 1998 Grammys, and was ranked # 12 on VH1's 100 Greatest Songs of the 90's.

Well, I'll stop because I'm still only on artists starting with letter "A" and this can only get worse...

Some other people try to solve this kind of problems with alcohol:

Wife: Look at that drunk guy.

Husband: who is he?

Wife: 10 yrs back he proposed to me & I rejected him.

Husband: Oh My God! He's still celebrating...

#101

25. SLEEP

(average recommended amount of sleep for adults is normally between 6-8 hours)

Many people we know don't sleep enough, and still they say they are not tired! That is not true. What's happening here is that these people became used to this state of "being tired" so they don't notice it as much (then over-compensate with caffeine). As soon as they wake up they are already in a state of high stress: Driving to work, If someone makes the smallest driving error it's enough to make this person explode, curse and scream. They have low energy levels, are tense, drink a lot of coffee, are very easy to irritate and have hard time to focus and perform.

YOU WOULDN'T LET THIS HAPPEN TO YOUR PHONE. DON'T LET IT HAPPEN TO YOU EITHER. SELF-CARE IS A PRIORITY, NOT A LUXURY !

The web page Everyday Health (www.everydayHealth.com) has a nice article:

"14 Seriously Amazing Reasons to Snag a Good Night's Sleep!" and mentioned in detail these points:

1. Lower Heart Attack Risk

2. Better Blood Pressure

3. Trimmer Waistline

4. More Energy

5. Happier Mood

6. Lower Diabetes Risk

7. Better Marriage

8. Better Sex Life

9. Glowing Skin

10. Stronger Immune System

11. Less Stress

12. Better Brainpower

13. Fewer Aches and Pains

14. Lower Cancer Risk

I think there are maybe one or two reasons here that might make it worth trying to sleep a little more 😊

26. DON'T COMPARE YOURSELF WITH OTHERS

With social media, comparing ourselves with others became a national sport. There is always someone much better than us in everything we do! There is always someone having, or pretending to have, a WONDERFUL time, while we are completely stuck in our non-exciting life.

I remember at a restaurant that I often go to, I saw this young couple having dinner without exchanging one single word. Then one suggested a selfie together, so they hugged each other and made a HUGE smile to post on Instagram, with a line like "the most romantic dinner"!
(maybe it was more romantic than other previous dinners because that silence, probably prevented many fights)

I know people (I can't say names 😊) who spend their time in restaurants just looking to find someone who is being served faster than our table!
Obviously this creates frustration and makes it quite difficult to feel happy during what could be a pleasant meal.

When my lovely nieces were younger I gave them three coins each under the table. One of them disguised well and smiled. The other waited a bit and before opening her hand, asked:
-Uncle, how much money did you give to my sister???

Every morning, very early, when I leave home I see Pedro sweeping the streets of the neigbourhood, always looking very happy. He makes a point of saying a loud and strong: "GOOD MORNING": Pedro likes to talk with all the neighbors who pass by, loves football and hard rock music. Pedro reminds me daily that it is possible to spend much more time in a good mood if we just stop constantly comparing our lives with the lives of others.

PLEASE, TURN-OFF THAT COMPARISON MACHINE!!!

"Don't compare yourself with other people; compare yourself with who you were yesterday."

Rule nº4 in Jordan Peterson´s BOOK: "12 Rules for Life- An Antidote to Chaos"

27. READ READ READ

(DON'T WAIT FOR MY NEXT BOOK!)

Aubrey Marcus, **(popular podcaster, author the New York Times Best-Selling author of "Own The Day, Own Your Life")** thoughts about not taking the easy way:

READING CAN SERIOUSLY DAMAGE YOUR IGNORANCE.

"The skill most important to acquire is what I call mental override.
It is the ability to override your thoughts and urges, take control of your body, and command the helm of your human starship."

Aubrey Marcus

#107

(Aubrey Marcus is another big fan of cold water showers, first thing in the morning, to sharpen that "mental override".)

The most successful entrepreneurs on the planet all maintain strong reading habits.
- **Bill Gates:** 50 books per year (in 2019 he had $104 billion in assets)
- **Warren Buffet:** 500 pages per day (in 2019 he had assets of $ 80 billion)

These are just two examples of thousands of successful men and women who mention reading as a critical success factor for them. But still, most of us still think that the easiest way is to play the lottery!

The website www.lifehack.org, is always full of interesting material, and published this:

"10 Benefits of Reading: Why You Should Read Every Day", mentioning,

1. **Mental stimulation**
2. **Stress reduction**
3. **Knowledge**
4. **Vocabulary expansion**
5. **Memory improvement**
6. **Stronger analytical thinking skills**
7. **Improved focus and concentration**
8. **Better writings Skills**
9. **Tranquility**
10. **Free entertainment**

OK, OK, you understand it is super important and has the potential to give you a life you dreamed of but can't have!! Well, think again. Here are my....

7 (+1) TIPS TO READ MORE:

1 - Carry a book with you at all times
2 - Choose very carefully what books you buy
3 - Put your mobile phone AWAY!
4 - Do NOT finish books you are not enjoying (don't feel guilty - burn them!)
5 - Schedule specific times to read
6 - Take breaks every 25 minutes
7 - Offer books to your friends (and they will offer books to you)

(+1) EXTRA Mile: check Tim Ferriss, teaching "Scientific Speed Reading: **How to Read 300% Faster in 20 Minutes**":
https://tim.blog/2009/07/30/speed-reading-and-accelerated-learning/

Please, don't tell me the lame excuse that you don't have time because just minutes ago you were watching television or looking at social media! Just read!!

(I know that sometimes laziness can strike...)

A GOOD BOOK

CAN CHANGE YOUR LIFE

"I do not think much of a man who is not wiser today than he was yesterday"

Abraham Lincoln

#109

28. EAT BETTER

(BABY STEPS)

I love all kinds of junk food, especially burgers, but I realized I prefer to stay in good shape and spend money on travel, rather than later having to spend it in on medicines.

So I took baby steps. I quit drinking Coke and started eating vegetables (a HUGE victory for me as someone who hated vegetables until I was 35!).

I stopped eating bread in the morning and ate eggs instead.

I became more interested in food with nutrients and looking for a balance (including supplementation) which can build my energy.

Still, there's a LONG way to go, but I am excited about improving this chapter and feeling such higher levels of energy. Ask help from a certified nutrition specialist.

" Don't step on it... It makes you cry "

#111

29. TIDY UP YOUR SPACE

I was always a little messy and deep down I think I even thought it was part of being macho 😊. Concepts like "Feng Shui" were for me an opportunity to laugh at those who preached them.
Until I read the book "Zen Habits" (Leo Babauta) which opened my eyes to the benefits of having my home organized, and my office table a little tidier (still a lot of work to do here ...).
A tidy space, without any doubt, emanates more harmony, less stress so we feel less rushed ...
Unlike in the past, I am now happy to get home because I find things tidy and more organized. Small daily efforts, just getting rid of non-essential items and clothes that haven't been worn for over two years can make a big difference.

REDUCE THE STRESS OF THE MESS

The worldwide famous Japanese Guru, tidying-up expert, **Marie Kondo** (wrote best-selling books like "The Life-Changing Magic of Tidying Up: The Japanese Art of Decluttering and Organizing.") was once asked why her work became so important for so many people, and she replied: **"I think it's because we not only have clutter in our homes but we also have clutter in our hearts."** (don't cry, please 😊)
This might be a bit sentimental but research shows that a cluttered space can also mean clutter in our minds! And, if that mess starts to get out of hand, it can lead to physical and mental health issues.

When it comes to deciding to get rid of stuff you have accumulated at home, the real question is: Is this **trash or treasure?**

Also, follow Marie Kondo´s Rule, ask yourself **"Does it spark joy?"**
(source: https://www.psycom.net/organize-clutter-mind-tidy-up)

#113

30. TAKE ACTION & DON'T GIVE UP...

Throughout life we always meet people who are difficult to impress, know everything, and have seen everything. Then we also realise that they are not successful in any aspect of life. They are average people who think they know everything and have become professional critics of everything.

"Knowledge in only Potential Power"

Napolean Hill, Book: "Think & Grow Rich"

Usually, they are very forthright on social media writing long opinionated posts.
·They are what Gary Vaynerchuk describes as "keyboard activists"!
The big difference from those who succeed is by **TAKING ACTION!**

With regards to NOT giving up we find excellent examples in many books. One example I particularly like is the book "Chicken Soup for the Soul" (Jack Canfield and Mark Hansen) which was rejected 144 times by publishers. But one day, after knocking on many doors, a publisher agreed to publish it and predicted that it would sell 20,000 copies. He was almost right 😊, Today it has sold 115 million copies. (I told you, being rejected pays-off big time, very soon it will be 1 million books per rejection!!)

The lesson that these people teach us is always the same, but it is worth saying again: The loser is not the one who falls or who fails, because the game only ends when we decide that the game is over! The loser is the one that quits.

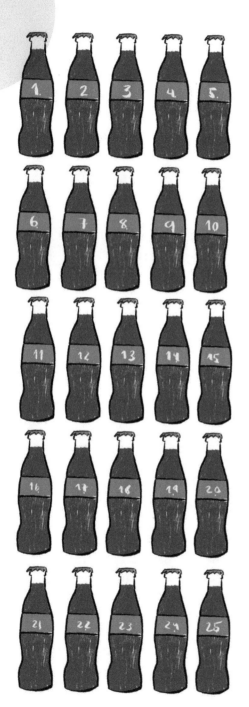

1 year

It reminds me of a football team I played in with friends when we were all in our 20s. We used to play against a team of older friends. Theoretically the game would be 90 minutes but, because they were older, they made the rules. I remember many times when the older guys were losing by 1 or 2 goals and we'd clearly played more than 90 minutes, but the game went on and on and on until... well, until they won it!

Tommy Baker, now a top-rated speaker, author and coach, performed a webinar early in his career with only 1 person attending! (By the way, it was his mum!) All successful people had a difficult start. This made them who they are. It's amusing to Google the very early days of successful people you admire. They all have one thing in common, the decision to change, the decision to take action daily!

"We are what we repeatedly do"

Will Durant

The month of December is usually filled with many dinners, parties and drinking. For me, in 2017 the month of December was difficult. A bit excessive, and so the Christmas party didn't finish well for me (not proud, long Story 😊)

It was the perfect timing, close to new year, when normally I made those cliché plans about the "new me"! (which never really happen!)

That's the time when Will Durant's quote came to mind. I realized I was partying way too much, and I didn't want to be a professional drinker anymore (although I had some talent) and made a decision to start training for a triathlon! A couple of months later I finished a long distance triathlon, but most of all I enjoyed a wonderful year practicing a new skill that made me stronger in many different ways.

When you want to quit something, it is always worth remembering the Chinese, **Jack Ma**, the founder of **Alibaba**, one of the biggest digital successes in the modern world, the richest man in China with a net worth of $ 25 billion.

Jack Ma's successive rejections and epic resilience:

- When the fast food chain, **KFC**, opened in his village, there were 24 candidates for 23 places. Jack was the one who was left out.
- **Local police** had 4 vacancies, there were 5 candidates....and Jack was excluded.
- He applied 10 times to **Harvard**. He was always rejected.

Many years later, the irony of fate was invited to speak at Harvard, where he left a recipe for success:

"Treat rejections as opportunities to learn and grow"

"We keep fighting. We keep changing ourselves, We don't complain" – Jack Ma

September 2017, Cascais, my 1st triathlon. IronMan 70,3 Cascais, without doubt one of the world's most stunning IronMan races in the world

#118

LEONARDO DA VINCCI:
4 years painting Mona Lisa and 25 years painting the masterpiece "Virgin of the Rocks"

The drummer of rock band, Def Leppard, Rick Allen, lost his left arm in a car accident. They told him that he would never play the drums again. Two years later, after an intense program of recovery and adaptation to a new drum model, he returned to the band and played over 30 years in packed concerts. Def Leppard sold over 100 Million Albums!

》》

(check Youtube, Def Leppard, Live, songs like "Animal" ; Let's get rocked; Hysteria)

"A quitter never wins, a winner never quits"

Napoleon Hill

Don't be afraid of critics. There will always be haters, and we should never allow these "people" to stop us. Harry Potter, one of the bestselling books of all time, with more than 400 million copies sold worldwide, and translated into 68 languages. Nevertheless, as I learned in a Seth Godin interview that, Harry Potter has more than a thousand ONE-star reviews.
More than one thousand people said, "This is the worst book I ever read in my life."
This is the price you must be prepared to pay when you start having some success. Learning to let go, is key to maintain some mental sanity.

HATERS

H: HAVING
A: ANGER
T: TOWARDS
E: EVERYONE
R: REACHING
S: SUCCESS

WHEN THINGS DON'T HAPPEN RIGHT AWAY JUST REMEMBER, IT TAKES 6 MONTHS TO BUILD A ROLLS-ROYCE AND 13 HOURS TO BUILD A TOYOTA.

31. WHAT'S YOUR ADVANTAGE?

Markus Buckingham and Donald O. Clifton, wrote an interesting book called **"Now discover your strengths".**
The key takeaways of this book are:
- We all have a combination of unique strengths.
- These natural skills are a competitive advantage over other people. We are naturally good at tasks related to these skills and of course we also just enjoy doing them. **We must focus all our energy on developing further these skills**
- To know what our strongest points are, please don't ask your mother. Instead you can find some serious online tests.

I particularly like the **Gallup Strengths Finder** available online for around $15 and takes less than an hour.
This test will generate a report some nice compliments, but, more importantly, your five strongest qualities. It will also indicate which sectors and tasks we should be focusing on.
It's very old-school (or silly, after reading this) to spend time trying to

"I FOUND SOMETHING I LOVE... AND NEVER GAVE UP"

Michael Phelps

#121

#122

improve our weaknesses.
The tasks related to our weaknesses must be allocated to those who are really strong in those areas. They must be delegated or outsourced. (even to your wife or husband)

Sometimes people need to go through truly difficult times to discover how much strength they really have, or to hit rock bottom in order to decide that they NEVER want to go through this situation.
Mark Johnson was addicted to heroin for almost 20 years. During his worst period, Mark needed £400 per day to feed his addiction.
When he hit the bottom, he found that only someone with a lot of inner strength could make £400 per day in such a deplorable state. He started putting this drive and energy into constructive things. Today he is the founder of a successful company, User Voice, which helps to integrate former prisoners into society.
(source: Book "The Idea in You" – Amor & Pellew)

"DECIDING WHAT NOT TO DO IS AS IMPORTANT AS DECIDING WHAT TO DO"

Steve Jobs

32. LOSERS HAVE GOALS, WINNERS HAVE SYSTEMS

Quote by Scott Adams

>>

#124

"AN IDIOT WITH A PLAN CAN BEAT A GENIUS WITHOUT A PLAN"

Warren Buffett

Stephen Covey has one of the most influential books ever written on personal transformation - **"7 Habits of Highly Effective People".**
It is one of those books that are worth reading several times because each time you read it you see different angles.
For some reason this book has sold over 15 million copies.
Each of the 7 habits described in the book deserved hundreds of pages and deep reflection.
All the 7 habits below were mentioned, one way or the other, by other authors.
But Stephen Covey's approach is incredibly inciteful and reading his book will give you a tool for life!

VERY briefly the principles are:
1 - **Be proactive**
2 - **Begin with the end in mind**
3 - **First things first**
4 - **Think win-win**
5 - **Seek first to understand, then to be understood**
6 - **Synergise!**
7 - **Sharpen the saw; growth**

Habit 1: **Be Proactive**

Recognize your **"Circle of influence"** and **"Circle of concern"**

Circle of concern: Don't just sit and wait for problems to happen
Circle of influence: constantly work to expand it! Take the initiative to react positively and improve the situation!
Take responsibility for what's happening.

Habit 2: **Begin with the end in mind**

"Envisage what you want in the future so you can work and plan towards it."
"All things are created twice. Before we act, we should act in our minds first."
Stephen suggests right at the beginning

"TO HELL WITH CIRCUMSTANCES I CREATE OPPORTUNITIES"

Bruce Lee

"**The average man is a conformist, accepting miseries and disasters with the stoicism of a cow standing in the rain.**"

Colin Wilson

"EFFORT AND COURAGE ARE NOT ENOUGH WITHOUT PURPOSE AND DIRECTION"

John F. Kennedy

#125

of the book that we must have the courage to write a **"Personal Mission Statement"**.

This manifesto is an exercise that helps us to understand what is really important. The suggestion is to focus on guiding principles. Not in people, nor in goods or activities that are too specific, since all of these are changeable over time.

Below is a brief outline of a personal mission statement that I loved:

I live in the present, wake up early and enjoy the day.
I focus on the essentials.
I strive to be an efficient person, planning smoothly and executing with energy.
I look at life with humor and don't take myself too seriously.
I try to listen more than I speak and always learn something new.
I give the best at home with joy.
I will do activities outside and surround myself with good people.
I always look on the bright side and am grateful for what I have.

Habit 3: **First Things First**

We should keep in mind and reflect on what is **important** and what is **urgent**! Bellow, the so called "Eisenhower Matrix" to help visualize and put some perspective:

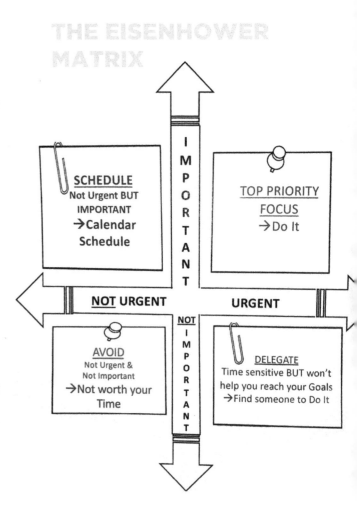

THE EISENHOWER MATRIX

In Quadrants № 1 and №4, for different reasons, you have easy decisions to make. In Quadrants № 2 and №3 it's a bit more difficult.

If you spend too much time doing things in Nº3, later you won't have time for the really important stuff. Nº4 its very tricky, because it is something non-urgent. If you are not careful and don't prioritise, then you might never do it! Careful: **"Stand by"** very often becomes **"Stand Bye Bye"**

To make it easier, some examples that I filled out below:

Habit 4: **Think Win-Win**

When we think long-term the **mutually beneficial solutions and agreements are always the best ones.** You might get away once with a selfish decision but, sooner or later, you might need that person. Neither is this is about being "nice", because the person (or company) you helped might come to save you later, just when you need it.

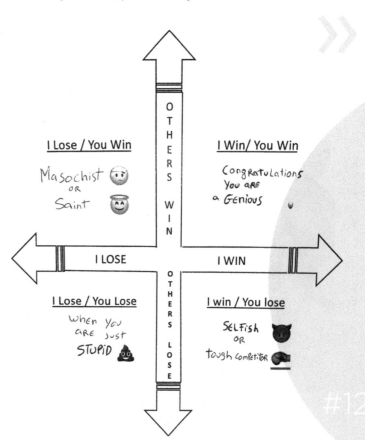

Writing this Book (took me 3 years)

MEEting with Bank to approve a Project 💰

NOT URGENT — URGENT

IMPORTANT / NOT IMPORTANT

Watching TV with Mother-In-Law

My BRother Calling for heLP with a Flat Tire

I Lose / You Win
Masochist
OR
Saint

I Win / You Win
Congratulations You aRE a Genious

OTHERS WIN / OTHERS LOSE

I LOSE — I WIN

I Lose / You Lose
when you aRE just STUPID 💩

I win / You lose
SELFish
OR
tough competitoR

#127

Habit 5: **Seek first to understand, then to be understood**

It's been mentioned many times. It looks so much easier than it really is.

"Most people do not listen with the intent to understand; they listen with the intent to reply."
Stephen R. Covey

"WHEN YOU TALK, YOU ARE ONLY REPEATING WHAT YOU ALREADY KNOW. BUT IF YOU LISTEN, YOU MAY LEARN SOMETHING NEW"

Dalai Lama

If we could just behave more often like this guy, above, you could have the world at your feet

Habit 6: **Synergise**

TeamWork, TeamWork, TeamWork, TeamWork

Even the greatest guys ever – whether in professional sport or business -know this!

When football superstar Cristiano Ronaldo was voted the world's best player in 2014, he bought each of his teammates an engraved personalized Bulgari watch worth around $10,000 each.

Michael Jordan

Michelangelo

Searching for **continuous improvement, balance and renewal** at different levels to keep high performance over many years.
..Physical renewal ⟶ Exercise
..Mental renewal ⟶ Yoga, meditation, prayer , good reading
..Spiritual renewal ⟶ service to society

Stephen Covey´s mentions the **"The Upward Spiral"** model.
It has 3 parts: **Learn, Commit, Do.**
Continuous improvement is valid both on a personal level but also withing the interpersonal spheres of influence.

Habit 7: **Sharpen the saw; growth**

You are work-in-progress improvement and renewal as a path of personal freedom, security, wisdom, and power.

Jack Nicholson

"Don't wish it were easier, wish you were better."

Jim Rohn

#129

33. AUTHENTICITY

BE YOURSELF; EVERYONE
ELSE IS ALREADY TAKEN

Oscar Wilde

Authenticity has become a key to personal and business success. Because being "authentic" means that we are original, different and unique. We know well that today's world depends on our ability, more than ever, to capture people's attention.

To be different you don't need to go as far as the charismatic rocker Alice Cooper, who at concerts wore a giant snake around his neck (please remember not to try this. By the way, one of his best songs is called "Hey Stupid"). Just be yourself and forget the easy route of copying everything and everyone!

Don't be an annoying copy cat!

In the film about Freddie Mercury and the British rock band, QUEEN, we clearly see the "turning point" from an unknown local band to become one of the best in music history. This was when the four members of the band refused the advice of their record company. Not following the same old path, just like other bands, and keeping their authenticity intact by making songs like "Bohemian Rhapsody". Initially criticized as being too long and quirky for a hit single, in December 2018 "Bohemian Rhapsody" became the most-streamed song from the 20th century, The number of downloads has now exceeded 1.6 billion.

Seth Godin, talks about this in his brilliant book **"Purple Cow"**.

Knowing that my sales team wouldn't read this book, I sent a summarised message in the mail below:

```
From: João Pinto Coelho
Sent: 6th November 2018 19:02
Subject: Will I stop the Car?

I was driving with a friend, through
the countryside. He saw a cow and
said:
"Stop the car because I see a cow
over there!"
THE END

Come on guys…..this was never going
to happen, nobody would ever stop the
car,
We've all seen a thousand cows! ☺
But we would have stopped the car if
we heard:
-Stop the car I see a purple cow over
there!
If we want to be noticed, we have to
be different.
What can we do differently… in the
individual business?
groups bookings?
customer experience?
marketing campaigns?
etc

──▶ This year let's dare to be
different and continue going the
extra mile!

PS- this week, some people came to
look at our Hotel and were amazed
by the SUGAR DRESSES designed by our
pastry chef Filipe
```

33. AUTHENTICITY

>>

> **"When writing the story of your life, don't let anyone else hold the pen"**

Harley Davidson

September 2015, Berlin, my first marathon. I was really happy with the result but my friends destroyed me because of my outfit. Apparently I was dressed as a tennis player, and not like a proper runner wearing lycra!

"I can't give you a sure-fire formula for success, but I can give you a formula for failure: try to please everybody all the time."

Herbert Bayard Swope

34. GROWING MINDSET

When the actor **Mathew McConaughey** was young he was asked the question:
Who is your hero?
He gave a very simple and unexpected answer:
- It's me in ten years
Ten years later, the same question came up, he answered:
- It's me in ten years
Although he was already successful and famous, he gave the exact same answer. He wanted more!

»

>>

Looking at so many people, famous, not famous, rich, poor, young, old, across many different cultures, there is little doubt that **improvement is the most exciting way to live your life!**
You have to believe that something different is coming, Otherwise life is boring .
You don't like changes ?
It's ironic that so many people say they don't like change or are scared of it, BUT when nothing changes they are bored and complain.

Tony Robbins, as usual, says is better:
"The Secret to REAL HAPPINESS is PROGRESS. Progress is equal to happiness. When we make progress in any areas of our lives on regular basis, we feel alive.
So we have to keep progressing in all aspects of our lives either emotional, spiritual, relationship or finance; and to make them better, we feel happy."
You know the secret - now WORK on it!!!!!
#QuitComplaining

THANK GOD IT'S **MONDAY** *with eric thomas*

To maintain your growth it's very important to know who to surround yourself with. Choose people who also aspire to grow and / or who you perceive to be better than you.
"YOU WILL BECOME LIKE THE FIVE PEOPLE YOU SPEND THE MOST TIME WITH" .
We don't know if it's 100% true, but we all know that our environmental conditions affect us directly and indirectly. We must not forget that even a good seed in bad soil will not bear much fruit.

RUN WITH THE CHEETAHS OR WALK WITH THE TURTLES ?
Remember that the most comfortable situations will not make us any better!

35. HAVE FUN

"NEVER UNDERESTIMATE THE IMPORTANCE OF HAVING FUN"

Randy Pausch (1960- 2008) on his farewell lecture when he was terminally ill with cancer

I

In 2019, according to U.S. Census Bureau show,
the average Retirement Age: 63
Life expectancy: 79
79 - 63 = 16 ⟶ Waiting for the last 16 years of your life to start enjoying ?
Do yourself a favor and find a way to enjoy your days before Retirement!
Why not enjoy 63 years + 16 years?

»

#136

»

For **Richard Branson** (Founder of Virgin Group, British magnate, investor, author and philanthropist) fun has always been the fuel to maintain enthusiasm and success in his work life:

"If you're not having fun, then it's probably time to call it quits and try something else."

Even in the very beginning of his business, with eminent financial problems, when things were very difficult, Richard Branson confirmed that same spirit:

"We were having such a great time that we kept going, mostly because we just liked hanging out together,"

In any part of your life, if you make a huge effort and you don't find a way to enjoy yourself, you will either quit or burnout!

A LITTLE PARTY
NEVER KILLED
NOBODY

Dad challenges kids to draw him sleeping so he can have a nap.

A sense of humour can get you out of even the most complicated situations. A young couple had been together for quite a long time, and so she started showing signs that she wanted to get married. But the guy "seemed" not to understand, which forced her to be more direct. She thought carefully about the words and told him:

- My love, we have been dating for a long time. I think this is the right time to take the next step. I want to dress in white.

So the guy replied:

- Ok you're right. Tomorrow I'm going to sign you up for karate classes!

Having fun, and sense of humor, not only opens the doors of creativity but also helps you sleep better:

Hey Gorgeous
- Wanna date me?
Yes = Smile
No = Backflip

#137

36. SIMPLICITY

"IT IS NICE TO BE IMPORTANT, BUT IT'S MORE IMPORTANT TO BE NICE"

John Templeton

In March 2019, **Anthony Joshua**, the world heavyweight boxing champion for the IBF, WBO and WBA, with accumulated prize money exceeding £50 million, opened the doors of the apartment where he was living 3 months before his world title defence. Surprisingly small, it had only two small rooms and was shared with a colleague. It had only a small toilet and kitchenette in one room and some old second-hand furniture.

Warren Buffet, in 2017, had $75 billion net worth, but still lived in the same simple house that he had bought in 1958 (by the way, he bought it for $31,000 and today it is worth about $270,000)

Rafael Santandreu, Spanish psychologist and author of several books on happiness, mentions 3 interesting points:

1. Transforming desires (or whims) into absolute needs is the fastest way to unhappiness!

2. The only real requirements for happiness: water and food.

3. Renunciation is what makes us strong, because if we really don't need anything we won't be afraid of losing anything......so we will live totally free.

The philosopher of **ancient Greece, Diogenes**, became voluntarily a beggar. He lived in a big barrel, like a dog ("the Dog" was one of his nicknames) and made his extreme poverty a virtue. He no longer needed comfort, status and was not concerned with his own physical safety.
(Diogenes lived 300 years before Christ. Following this many showed their strength through renunciation, through simplicity, like Gandhi and Mother Teresa of Calcutta)

"SIMPLICITY IS THE KEY TO BRILLIANCE"

Bruce Lee

#139

In this chapter about simplicity, there is no better example than children. As I have a large family and many nephews and nieces, I receive daily lessons on this subject.

I asked a niece to tell me about what would be her dream day.... what would be the perfect day, a day where she could have ANYTHING. I said that there were no restrictions whatsoever!
She replied that she wanted to play with her brother in the morning, have lunch with her parents at "Burger King" and go to the pool with some friends.

When my sister was 10 years old, her grandfather asked her affectionately how old she thought he was. She replied: "I think you are about 100 or 200 years old! "

We have to be like children:
- **No fear of the truth:** It was a child who cried out: "The Emperor has no clothes"
- **Persistent:** they are able to ask something 1000 times until they get it!
- **Dreamers:** imagination without limits!
- **Focused:** when they are playing, they put 100% focus in that task.
- **Light-hearted:** easy smile and love to play.

You were a child who fell of your bike thousands of times and kept getting back on it until you could ride it .We cannot give up being that child!

DON'T GROW UP IT'S A TRAP

37. DO SOMETHING EXTRA

Super-athlete David Goggins says several times that it is easy to stand out in today's world because most people are average, and we got used to "average" being OK.

We often praise people saying, "he is a normal person" as if it was excellent to be another one of the crowd. The point is, today, if you do a little extra it´s easy to stand out from the rest of the crowd.

It's worth mentioning the book "Keep Going" from Austin Kleon, where it says:

THE ORDINARY + EXTRA ATTENTION = EXTRAORDINARY

I thought a bit more about this (I know it doesn't sound like me) and added the following below:

Ordinary + Extra Work = ExtraOrdinary

Ordinary + Extra Patience = ExtraOrdinary

Ordinary + Extra Practice = ExtraOrdinary

Ordinary + Extra Reading = ExtraOrdinary

Ordinary + Extra Networking = ExtraOrdinary

Ordinary + Extra Hours = ExtraOrdinary

Ordinary + Extra Gym = ExtraOrdinary

Ordinary + EXTRA Something = ExtraOrdinary!!!

The point is ⟶ don't be just Ordinary
DO SOMETHING EXTRA!!!!

YESTERDAY
YOU SAID
TOMORROW

JUST DO IT.

NEVER GIVE UP HOPE
THIS GUY MARRIED
BEYONCÉ.

#143

After finishing this book (👏 thanks) you
may think I'm strong and confident!
(there was good level of me bragging
and also carefully chosen photos)
Nothing could be further from the truth,
this book could be called:
37 tricks to combat my
vulnerabilities and insecurities
(that arise daily!)

A wonderful quote:

"Your mind is a garden. Your thoughts are the seeds. You can grow flowers or you can grow weeds."

For me the most important reminder
here is: weeds have to be pulled out
every day!!
There are so many days that I feel like I'm
not good enough.
And others I feel worst 💩

The list of insecurities that I feel or felt is endless, below I share a few:
- at school I had a high pitched voice, lasted until 18 years old (an endless desert)
- I was skinny, easily intimidated by stronger guys
- I was quickly annoyed specially when things started to go wrong (I even broke some tennis rackets)
- I was given big head start by a generous father and felt I was not living to my true potential
- often felt incompetent, working with family business that went through substantial financial difficulties
- Many times felt I was not leading by example
- Not having the courage to tell people what I really think
- being too nice and far from assertive
- losing hair
- getting older
- etc etc etc (trust me!)

We can have a giant capacity to destroy ourselves, to find ourselves ridiculous! Sometimes we even think that everyone is laughing at us.
On the glorious day, my TV stopped working 📺, I had nothing better to do than starting to read a little more...
Daily discipline and rituals together with some rules reduced my feelings of insecurity and made me feel a little stronger.
Suddenly I started to enjoy some small victories in different chapters of my life....
Some of this achievements passed an image that I was a confident and secure person.

In fact, I was not that person, I was indeed confident but just during that moment. A few hours after I felt vulnerable again!
it was time to reload with another injection of confidence, with more reading, routines, rituals!
These 37 rules are daily pills I need to take often!
As I started feeling the results of personal growth and saw positive changes happening, I wanted to share with everyone who also feel far from their true potential!
If at least one or two of these 37 rules help you, I will be very Happy!
Your Mindset can Make You Or Break You .
Take care of your garden and beautiful things will start growing!
Remember your family needs you stronger, your friends need you to be stronger, your company and country too!
Feel free to read this book again but mainly to buy another book to offer a friend.
100% of profits go to charity (support the Children in Kenya)!!

THANK YOU
João

👥 Special Thanks to:
.Cat Rao: Character Designer (@cat.rao)
.Rui Camacho: graphics & book pagination
.Francisco Cyrne: advisor for Creative Design
.Andy Barwell and Susan Conde: for making my English look decent
.António Pinto Coelho: for all the help, building the idea, and then giving up 😊

ISBN: 978-84-685-5706-9

FINAL MESSAGE:

"Let no one ever come to you without leaving happier"

Mother Teresa

SOME BOOKS I REALLY ENJOYED:

CREATIVITY
Steal Like an Artist – Austin Kleon
The Art of Creative Thinking– Rod Judkins
Ignore Everybody– Hugh MacLeod
Daily Rituals: How Artists Work – Mason Currey

INNOVATION
Practically Radical – William Taylor
Weird Ideas That Work – Robert I. Sutton
Creative Confidence – David and Tom Kelley
The Art of Possibility – Rosamund Zander and
Benjamin Zander

BRANDING
This Is Marketing – Seth Godin
Unlabel – Marc Ecko
Turning Intelligence into Magic– Hegarty
Ogilvy on Advertising – David Ogilvy

ENTREPRENEURSHIP
The 4-Hour Workweek – Timothy Ferriss
Think and Grow Rich – Napoleon Hill
Crush It!: Why Now is the Time to Cash in on Your
Passion – Gary Vaynerchuk
Do Cool Sh*it – Miki Agrawal

PERSONAL CHANGE
Tools of Titans – Tim Ferriss
The Miracle Morning – Hal Elrod
Awaken the Giant Within – Anthony Robbins
Atomic Habits – James Clear
The Power of Habit – Charles Duhigg
The Good Psychopath's Guide to Success – Andy
McNab
Habit Stacking: 97 Small Life Changes That Take Five
Minutes or Less – S.J. Scott
F**k It - Do What You Love – John C. Parkin
Own the Day, Own Your Life – Aubrey Marcus
Man's Search for Meaning — Viktor Frankl
The Monk Who Sold His Ferrari — Robin Sharma
The 7 Habits of Highly Effective People - Stephen
Covey
High Performance Habits – Brendon Burchard
The Power of Positive Thinking – Norman Vincent
Peale

BUSINESS
Re-imagine! – Tom Peters
Funky Business - Jonas Ridderstråle & Kjell
Nordström
Punk Marketing – Richard Laermer & Mark Simmons

TIME MANAGEMENT
Eat that Frog – Brian Tracy
Essentialism: The Disciplined Pursuit of Less – Greg
McKeown

GOLF
Zen Golf- Dr. Joseph Parent;
Golf Is Not a Game of Perfect– Bob Rotella

ZEN (for Beginners) & Inner Peace
Zen Habits – Leo Babauta
Zen Happens - Dan Manning
Calm: Calm the Mind. Change the World – Michael
Acton Smith
The Power of Now: A Guide to Spiritual
Enlightenment – Eckhart Tolle
Think Like a Monk – Jay Shetty
Stillness Is the Key - Ryan Holiday

SALES
To Sell Is Human – Daniel H. Pink
Swim with the sharks without being eaten alive –
Harvey Mackay
SPIN Selling -Neil Rackham
The 48 Laws of Power – Robert Greene
Influence: The Psychology of Persuasion – Robert B.
Cialdini

INTERNET STRATEGY
Youtility – Jay Bier
Free – Chris Anderson
Epic Content Marketing – Joe Pulizzi

SPORTS & Persistence
No sé donde está el límite pero si sé donde no está –
Josef Ajram
Can't Hurt Me: Master Your Mind and Defy the Odds
– David Goggins
Run or Die – Kilian Jornet

UNDERSTANDING OTHERS
The Enneagram Made Easy: Discover the 9 Types of
People   -Renee Baron
The Four Agreements: A Practical Guide to Personal
Freedom – Don Miguel Ruiz

PUBLIC SPEAKING
Talk like TED: Carmine Gallo

#147

37

HACKS FOR PERSONAL GROWTH

CPSIA information can be obtained
at www.ICGtesting.com
Printed in the USA
BVHW021003051021
618192BV00021B/687